walking easy

in the

San Francisco

Bay Area

Wendy Logsdon &
Roger Rapoport

GATEWAY
B O O K S

Printed in the United States of America

Gateway Books
Oakland, CA

Distributed by Publishers Group West

Library of Congress Cataloging-in-Publication Data

Logsdon, Wendy, 1968-
    Walking easy in the San Francisco Bay Area / Wendy Logsdon & Roger
  Rapoport.
      p.   cm.
    Includes index.
    ISBN 0-933469-20-9
    1. Hiking—California—San Francisco Bay Area—Guidebooks.
  2.Walking—California—San Francisco Bay Area—Guidebooks. 3.San
  Francisco Bay Area—Guidebooks. I. Rapoport, Roger, 1946-
  GV199.42.C22S26946 1996
  917.94'6—dc20   95-6502
                                                          CIP

Acknowledgements

We gratefully acknowledge the assistance of the California State Parks and Recreation Department, the Golden Gate National Recreation Area, the East Bay Regional Park District, and numerous other county and local park agencies who assisted us on the research for this book. Andrew Head, Kathryn Campaigne, Debi Dunn, Chris Rovee, Donna Lee, Amanda Estes, Bonnie Smetts, Jesse McKinney, and especially our publishers, Judy and Don Merwin, all smoothed the path to publication. To all of them we say thanks for making our journey a pleasure.

CONTENTS

This book is dedicated to
Laurie Forrest Logsdon and Dan Rapoport

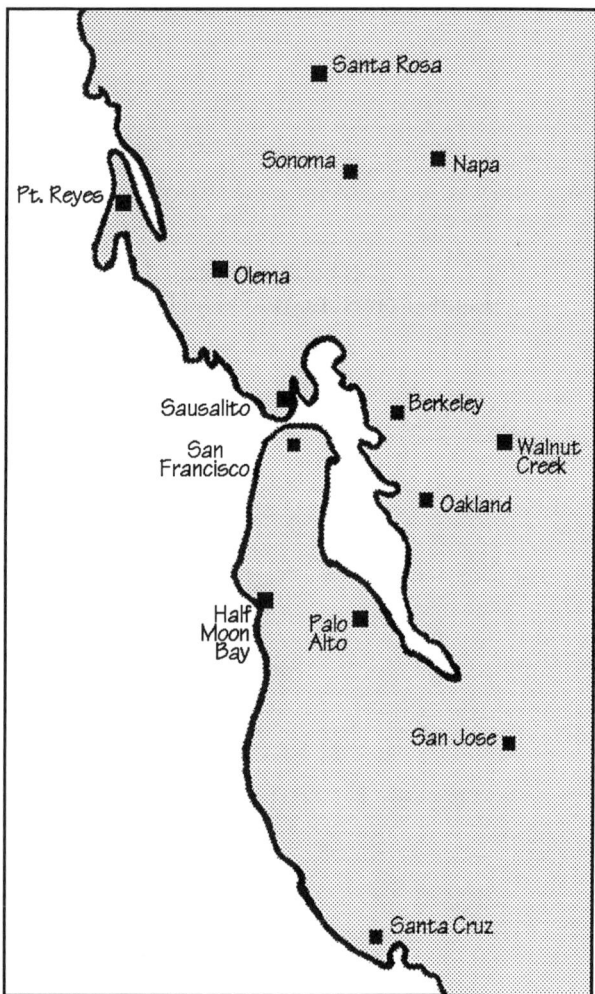

Santa Rosa

Sonoma

Napa

Pt. Reyes

Olema

Sausalito

Berkeley

San Francisco

Walnut Creek

Oakland

Half Moon Bay

Palo Alto

San Jose

Santa Cruz

BECOMING AN *EASY WALKER*

San Francisco, the city of restaurants and romance, is famous for its steep hills, soaring bridges, and classic cable cars—the urban experience where culture and commerce thrive side by side. Most overlook, however, a unique feature of this region—a semi-wilderness at its door-step. The rugged, wind-swept cliffs, lofty mountains, soft and seamless rolling hills, and towering redwoods comprise the wilderness that frames this vibrant city.

As walking increasingly becomes the most popular form of recreation in the United States, San Francisco and its neighboring counties naturally cater to this trend, thanks to national, state, regional, and county park systems. Circling the region is the Bay Area Ridge Trail—a 400 mile long route comprised of a series of hiking trails looping around the San Francisco Bay. This route, created by San Francisco and its neighboring counties, reflects the region's appreciation of rural splendor in an urban setting, as well as its acute desire to preserve the area's valuable wilderness from further development.

This book is designed for "active" visitors of all ages who enjoy the outdoors and want to experience the area's natural environment and its cultural offerings. It is also a handy companion for locals searching for a one-day escape. A helpful resource to the Bay Area's many walking opportunities, this conveniently sized book details some of the region's most beautiful parks.

In addition to detailing 39 walks in 32 parks, supplementary information on accommodations, restaurants, and sights in each county or Bay region is included.

Divided into four sections, this book covers San Francisco and its bordering counties north, east, and southern sections. Walks in Marin, Sonoma, and Napa counties are featured in the

North Bay chapter, while East Bay walks include Alameda and Contra Costa counties, as well as San Mateo, Santa Cruz, and Santa Clara counties to the south.

Walks include parks and rural areas within each county. With each walk we also provide descriptive and background information on the park and include directions to get there. A variety of different terrain ranging from easy strolling to challenging hikes is recommended.

Each walk is rated. **Gentle** refers to wider paths, shorter walking time and relatively little change in elevation. Longer walks that include more substantial climbing are rated **Comfortable. More Challenging** walks are lengthy. They include steep ascents and descents and should be attempted by those in good shape. Personally tested by the authors, each of these walks range from 30 minutes to five hours. All can be done in one day.

Trails mentioned here are well signposted but we've included sketch maps which provide a general idea of the route you'll be taking. We recommend picking up a park brochure or map to supplement this book. These are usually located at park headquarters, visitor centers, or ranger stations.

> ☞ **HINT: Most parks featured in this book offer free maps, with the exception of State Parks which charge a small fee for their maps.**

Selected walks in this book vary from San Francisco coastal or bayshore strolls to East Bay oak woodlands—a chaparral wilderness found throughout the Bay Area. Walks also dot the coast from the North Bay and south to San Mateo and the Santa Cruz mountains, leading through majestic redwood forests—a unique asset of this region nurtured by the fog belt.

Timing is Everything

One of the great pleasures of San Francisco and the Bay Area is its temperate climate which makes visiting and spending time outdoors pleasant any time of the year. Beside walking, there are plenty of other activities to keep you busy and comfortable. The temperature, varying little with the seasons, is moderately cool in the city and along the coast, (54-65 in summer, 49-59 in winter) with inland regions colder in winter and considerably warmer in summer.

The maritime climate is influenced primarily by the region's proximity to the ocean. Fog, common in the summer months, is created by the clash of the warm and cold ocean currents.

The Bay Area has two, rather than four, seasons: the rainy season between October and April and the dry season the rest of the year.

Spring and Autumn are undoubtedly the best months for walking in the Bay Area. Spring is susceptible to showers but worth the visit as the hillsides are a vibrant green. Blue and yellow lupine and bright orange California poppies carpet the hillsides. The crisp, cool climate at this time of the year also makes for comfortable *Easy Walking.*

Early Autumn sees little rain and fewer crowds, but remember, the warmer climate in September and October also means a ten to 20 degree temperature increase in the Bay Area's inland regions. To avoid the heat, plan on hitting the trails in the early morning or late afternoon. This way *Easy Walkers* can comfortably enjoy the harvest yellows, oranges, and reds painting the forests before leaves fade away.

Although there is less daylight for walking and showers are common, some of the most sparkling and spectacular views of the Bay are seen in the winter months.

During the summer, the city and coast are frequently blanketed by fog, while inland valleys are customarily dry and hot. Keep in mind that the heart of the summer season also brings out the tourist crowds. Be prepared!

☞ **HINT: For a daily weather forecast, check the local paper or dial 936-1212.**

Arriving by Air

Three different airports serve the Bay Area. The largest and most congested, **San Francisco International Airport**, or SFO, is located 14 miles south of San Francisco in San Mateo County. Frequent shuttle and taxi service connects travelers between the airport and downtown San Francisco. Most foreign travelers will arrive at this airport.

Oakland International Airport is smaller and substantially more convenient. A short BART (Bay Area Rapid Transit) ride connects this airport with downtown San Francisco and many East Bay locations.

San Jose International Airport, 50 miles south of San Francisco, may be a good choice if you're planning to begin your tour of the Bay Area and its walking pleasures in the foothills of the Santa Clara Valley or the Santa Cruz Mountains.

> ☞ **HINT: Phone numbers for airports: SFO (415) 761-0800, OAK (510) 577-4000, SJC (408) 277-4759. Phone numbers for airport shuttles: SFO Airporter (415) 673-2432; Super Shuttle (415) 558-8500; Bayporter Express (415) 467-1800.**

Arriving by Train/Bus

There's been a resurgence in train travel over the last few years. If you have the time to make the journey to the Bay Area part of your vacation, **Amtrak** offers relaxed and scenic journeys from across the nation. The main train terminal is located across the Bay in Emeryville where a shuttle transports visitors into the city. (A new terminal is now under construction in Oakland). For information and reservations call (800) 872-7245.

Greyhound and other commercial bus lines service San Francisco as well as other major cities in the Bay Area. The main bus terminal in San Francisco is located downtown at the Transbay Bus Terminal. Greyhound has its own terminal in the city and also offers service to Transbay. (Greyhound: (800) 231-2222.)

Public Transportation in the City and Beyond

In compact San Francisco, public transportation is the easiest way to get around while driving a car is an unnecessary nuisance. **BART**, the Bay Area's subway system, is clean and comfortable but unfortunately it has only one line running between the East Bay and the city. Within the city BART transports visitors to the Financial District, Union Square, and the Civic Center areas. Unfortunately it doesn't serve most other neighborhoods that you might visit during your stay.

San Francisco Municipal Railway (MUNI) operates the city's streetcars, buses, and cable cars, while providing transportation from several San Francisco BART stations to other areas throughout the city.

> ☞ **HINT: Senior citizens only pay $ .35 for every ride taken on MUNI, including transfers. Available to all commuters is Muni's Fast Pass which offers unlimited service for $35 a month. Seniors pay just $8. Fast Passes can be purchased from the visitor information center in Hallidie Plaza or from outside vendors such as hotels, supermarkets, and shops.**

> ☞ **HINT: Bart also offers discounts for seniors. Riders 65 or older can purchase a green BART card from public venues such as shops or hotels and get $16 worth of transportation for only $1.60.**

> ☞ **HINT: No trip to San Francisco is complete without a ride on one of the city's classic cable cars. Dating back to 1873, they continue to transport visitors and locals to the Financial District, North Beach, Nob Hill, and Fisherman's Wharf.**

MUNI transport provides access to most locations but can be tedious. Taxis are quicker and less hassle but, of course, much more expensive.

Attention *Easy Walkers*: San Francisco is a pedestrian city. While visiting, make a point of walking—it is definitely the best way to experience this city's charm. The hills, a refreshing challenge, offer unique Bay vistas. Walking is also the best way to explore San Francisco's ethnic neighborhoods.

Commuting via public transport to the rest of the Bay Area can be a challenge. Public Transport is available from the city to areas beyond the Bay, for example **CalTrain** is a shuttle train connecting San Francisco with San Jose and the South Bay, and the **ferry** system is a refreshing way to explore the North and East bays. Unfortunately, many of the parks we have recommended are scattered in remote areas which are not convenient to public transport. Although we mention public transportation whenever possible, we strongly recommend renting a car when venturing beyond the city.

BART: (415) 788-BART
MUNI: (415) 637-MUNI

Taxi Cabs:
Yellow Cab: (415) 626-2345
DeSoto Cab: (415) 673-1017
Luxor Cab: (415) 282-4141

Ferry Companies:
Red and White Fleet: (800) BAY CRUISE
                          (San Francisco/Tiburon and Vallejo)
Blue & Gold Fleet: (510) 522-3300
                          (San Francisco/East Bay)
Golden Gate Transit: (415) 332-6600
                          (San Francisco/Sausalito and
                          Larkspur)

Rental Car Agencies:
Alamo: (800) 327-9633
Avis: (800) 331-1212
Hertz: (800) 654-3131
National: (800) 227-7368

☞ **HINT: Most rental car agencies are based at or near the airports. Many offer discounts for seniors, but con-**

ditions and deductions vary depending on the company, so shop around.

Accommodations

From budget lodging to Five Star accommodations, San Francisco will make any guest feel at home. We recommend intimate, homey places—small inns and Bed and Breakfasts—that fit a moderate budget. These comfortable choices are convenient to all of the walks and sights recommended in this book.

Bed and Breakfast accommodations offer a personal touch. Hosts, friendly and helpful, are eager to provide their guests with specifics about the area—worthy sights, restaurants which fit your mood and budget, as well as authentic delis or gourmet markets where *Easy Walkers* can purchase a picnic lunch or snack.

☞ HINT: Ask your Bed & Breakfast host about midweek discounts, especially during the off season.

☞ HINT: Don't be caught off guard: Many Bay Area Bed & Breakfast Inns require a two night minimum stay on weekends and sometimes longer on holiday weekends.

☞ HINT: To preserve period antiques which commonly grace interiors, and for the comfort and consideration of other guests, a No Smoking policy exists at many Bed & Breakfasts.

☞ HINT: If you're having a hard time finding accommodations, reservation services, such as Bed & Breakfast International (P.O. Box 282910, San Francisco 94128; (415) 696-1690), have listings for over 450 B & Bs, small inns, and hostels.

Dining in and around San Francisco

Easy Walkers visiting San Francisco are in for an unforgettable culinary experience. The sheer number of restaurants in the city and its neighboring counties reflects this region's appreciation of quality cuisine.

While this is *the* home of California Cuisine—that subtle, experimental twist to standard fare, which insists on using fresh, locally grown ingredients, great ethnic food is also easy to find. The Bay Area's vast ethnic community supports a wide array of restaurants offering authentic Italian cuisine, Ethiopian fare, and the far reaching flavors of Burma. With dozens of nationalities represented, you can easily sample fine regional cooking from all over the world.

Regional Specialties

San Francisco is distinguished for neighborhoods such as the North Beach Italian community, Japan Town, and Chinatown. Each is equally famous for its ethnic cuisine.

Known for its exotic cultural festivals, the Bay Area has also helped shape culinary trends. Here steak and potatoes are not king. The local culinary revolution began in Berkeley in the early 1960s, under the guiding influence of Alice Waters. Her restaurant, Chez Panisse, has dazzled diners for years with a menu dedicated to locally grown ingredients. Many of Waters's tutees have furthered this tradition, experimenting with innovative flavors and presentations.

A healthy and fruitful restaurant rivalry is complemented by the region's excellence in other areas, such as wine making and baking. East Bay specialty bread makers, such as the Acme Bakery, Metropolis, and Grace Baking, keep many venerable Italian North Beach bakeries on their toes. San Francisco's Sourdough bakeries, such as Boudin, are also worth a try. A natural leavener, sourdough has been used since biblical times to make light bread. Until the development of commercial yeast, it was the only way to make leavened bread.

☞ **HINT: Pick up some freshly baked Bay Area bread in the local specialty market (ask your hotel or Bed &**

Breakfast proprietor). Try it with Sonoma Jack or a local goat cheese. It's perfect for picnics planned around the easy walks in this book.

Wine from Napa and Sonoma County is one of the region's great pleasures. Just head an hour north of San Francisco and find yourself transported to another land altogether, graced with vineyards attached to wineries dating back to the late 1800s. Here you'll find Cabernets, Chardonnays, and other imported varietal wines that have put California wines on par with European wines.

☞ **HINT: Zinfandel, the only grape native to California, blends to create a smooth, spicy flavored wine. Unlike most heavy reds, it can be enjoyed with almost any meal. Not to be confused with the sweeter white Zinfandel, Napa's red is making a welcome comeback.**

☞ **HINT: While Napa and Sonoma county wines are well known, visitors are surprised to learn that wineries dot the entire bay region. Grapes are cultivated in the Santa Cruz mountains, Santa Clara Valley, and in the nether regions of the East Bay.**

While the Bay Area produces millions of gallons of wine each year, it also hand selects and imports some of the worlds best and most flavorful coffee beans. Very black, very strong, and, most importantly, very tasty, Bay Area folks know their coffee and they know the best. That is why many drink Peet's coffee. The coffee is so popular that now you can find Peet's coffee houses throughout the area. But Peet's is just one of the best. Simply frequent any cafe in Berkeley or North Beach, and you won't be disappointed.

Where to Eat and Drink

San Francisco and the Bay Area has more restaurants and eateries per capita than any other region in America. Narrow down your choices by ethnicity and price range. We've already suggested staying in moderate inns or Bed and Breakfasts which usually provide your first meal of the day. Proprietors can also recommend nearby places to eat and drink.

In each section we offer a number of dining suggestions. If you enjoy coffee, as do many Bay Area locals, we list some morning and evening cafes, as well as specialty markets whereby you can shop for picnic fare.

> ☞ HINT: Local papers and magazines such as *San Francisco Focus* provide a rundown of particular restaurants in the area. Also try the *San Francisco Chronicle* or *Examiner*, the *San Jose Mercury News*, *Oakland Tribune*, the *Marin Independent Journal*, or the *Contra Costa Times*.

What to Wear

Boots - Sturdy hiking boots are essential for *Easy Walking* in the Bay Area which covers a variety of terrain. Please don't substitute boots with running shoes. While some consider tennies a suitable alternative, they don't provide nearly enough grip or needed ankle support in terrain with unsure footing. Don't skimp on this purchase. Plan to spend a considerable sum. Shop around your local recreation and sporting goods stores. Since there are a variety of styles for different types of hiking and backpacking, you'll want to be sure your choice is practical and comfortable.

Socks - Two pairs of socks: a synthetic liner with a heavy wool or cotton outer layer are recommended.

Pants - Long pants, particularly denim, to protect your legs from poison oak, unfriendly bugs and critters, low branches, and prickly shrubs that extend onto walking paths. On warm days, you'll prefer comfortable shorts. Just be sure you can avoid poison oak. Remember also to check yourself and your partner for ticks after each day's walk.

> ☞ HINT: Upper body wear varies according with the Bay Area's unpredictable weather. Cold, foggy mornings can give way to sunny, scorching afternoons. Prepare yourself by dressing in layers.

Shirts - Short-sleeve, cotton T-shirts are a comfortable base layer. On top of this you may consider wearing a long-sleeve flannel or denim shirt which still provides warmth but is light weight and easy to tie around the waist.

Sweaters/Sweatshirts - These provide extra warmth, but can be cumbersome once the sun appears.

Wind breaker/rain jacket - This is another "must" item all year round. It stores easily in your backpack when not in use.

> ☞ **HINT: Our hiking apparel suggestions are also recommended for touring the Bay Area.**

Plan on also bringing a slightly heavier coat for cool evenings. Keep in mind that dining in the Bay Area can be a special occasion. Formal attire is not required, but nice, comfortable slacks, with a turtleneck, and/or sweater is an appropriate outfit for both men and women.

Backpack - One light day pack is often sufficient for two people. Make sure it's sturdy and fits comfortably. Padded straps provide additional comfort and are definitely recommended. New hightech models with pocket compartments and additional straps that form the pack to your back are also well worth the investment.

Fannypack - Perfect for small essential items such as car keys and extra money. This is a nice accompaniment if you're not the one carrying the backpack.

Smaller items to bring, in addition to your *Walking Easy* guidebook, are an address book, aspirin, bandana, binoculars, camera, coin change, compass, credit card, small first aid kit with moleskin for blisters, small flashlight, hat or sun visor, identification card or drivers license, insect repellent, pocket tissues, prescription medicines, road map of the Bay Area, small sewing kit, sun glasses, sun screen, Swiss army knife, and whistle.

EASY WALKERS' PACKING CHECKLIST

_____bandana or scarf
_____bathing suit
_____belt
_____blouse
_____coat, casual or dress
_____hat
_____jacket, rain or windbreaker
_____pajamas/night gown
_____pants, hiking
_____shirts, long-sleeved flannel, turtleneck, and
          T-shirts
_____shoes, hiking, casual, and dress
_____shorts, hiking and casual
_____slacks, casual or dress
_____slippers
_____socks, hiking and dress
_____sweater
_____sweatshirt
_____undergarments

For Your Information—From Telephones to Tipping

Earthquakes - Earthquakes come with the territory in California. In the Bay Area there are three major fault lines: the San Andreas, a part of which runs near Point Reyes, the Hayward Fault in the East Bay and the Calaveras fault.

Protect yourself in one of three ways. If an earthquake occurs while you're inside, find protective, sturdy cover such as a doorway, table, or bed. Avoid being near windows that shatter or furniture that can topple, such as bookshelves. When outside, find an open space away from structures or power lines. If you're driving, park on the side of the road and remain inside.

Geography - Located on the far west and northern coast of California, adjacent to the Pacific Ocean, the Bay Area features a varied coastal geography characterized by rocky shores, sandy beaches, offshore rocks and islands, marine terraces, estuaries, rivers and streams, and coastal mountain ranges. Inland valleys, formed by gaps within the coast ranges, dot the region as well, but the most prominent geographic feature of this area is, of course, the Bay, with a surface area totaling 460 square miles.

Insurance - If a last minute illness prevents your journey, **Travel Guard** (800-826-1300) provides trip cancellation insurance. The charge is only $5.50 for every $100.00 of coverage.

Medical Evacuation Insurance from **Travel Assistance International** (800-368-7878) is offered to foreigners traveling within the United States. They will arrange hospital treatment in case of serious illness, or, in special circumstances, fly you to a hospital in your own country.

Medical Care - Getting ill or injuring yourself in a foreign or unfamiliar city can create added anxiety. Fortunately San Francisco has established several referral services to point you in the right direction. **Doctor referral service** (415) 561-0853; **Dental referral service** (415) 421-1435.

> ☞ HINT: Although these services cover primarily the San Francisco area, they can refer you to other services throughout the Bay Area.

Medications - In the case of loss, theft, or if, for some reason, your return trip is delayed, wise travelers should always bring a written copy of their prescriptions (that includes prescriptions for glasses too). Also make sure you carry prescription and non prescription drugs, such as aspirin or allergy tablets, nearby in your purse, backpack, or carry-on luggage. This will protect you against mishandling of your checked luggage.

> ☞ HINT: Traveler's Aid Society offers assistance in the case of lost plane tickets, hotel difficulties, or even lost

companions. (415) 255-2252 (in the East Bay: (510) 444-6834).

Newspapers - The *San Francisco Chronicle* is your main link to newsworthy events while you're in San Francisco. The *San Francisco Examiner* is the other big city paper. Sunday's paper is a joint effort between the two and, if you're visiting, is a worthy investment. There is no avoiding the "Pink Section," listing arts, entertainment, and events information for the upcoming week which visitors should find extremely helpful.

Marin County is serviced by the *Marin Independent Journal* which, while covering mainstream news, maintains more of a local slant, while the East Bay's much larger *Oakland Tribune* has emerged from its past financial woes as a member of the Alameda newspaper group. Finally, the *San Jose Mercury News* offers good coverage of the Bay Area scene.

Radio - Easy listening in San Francisco and the Bay Area is on the wane. Recently one of the area's best loved stations, KJAZ, which served jazz aficionados for over 35 years, went cable as a result of financial difficulties. The favorite classical station is KKHI (100.7), or you can hear pre-recorded classics on KDFC (102.1). Meanwhile, new rock stations seem to spring up effortlessly. For mellow and classic rock tunes, turn to KFOG (104.5) which is always pleasing.

NPR addicts, fear not, you can sate your fix by turning to its local station KQED (88.5) which tenuously remains on the air through listener support. Public and nonprofit radio is also heard on KPFA (94.1) and KALW (91.7). Finally, while transporting yourself throughout the Bay Area, highway conditions and traffic information is available around the clock on AM station KCBS (740). The city's leading talk-stations are KGO (810) and KSFO (560).

Trail Safety - Although unpleasant, it's necessary to mention specifics that require particular caution during your Bay Area stay. First and foremost, tell someone, be it park ranger, hotel or Bed & Breakfast proprietor, or a relative back home, where you are going for the day. Crime on Bay Area Trails is rare but has been known to occur. Protect yourself here, as on trails anywhere, by bringing along a whistle, personal alarm, or walking stick.

Insects and animals also pose a threat to *Easy Walkers*. Parklands, especially inland areas, are heavily populated with yellow jackets. Particularly in the summer and autumn months they nest underground near trails. This is a good reason to remain on designated walkways. Brightly colored clothing, perfumes, and strong scented lotions attract these buzzing buggers. If one of them decides to land on you, it's best to blow, rather than swat, away.

The Bay Area also shelters ticks. Only one of 49 species in the Bay Area, the Western Black-legged Tick, has been known to transmit Lyme disease which, if detected early, causes little harm. Avoid straying from main walking path onto grassy areas where ticks are likely to be found. Long sleeved shirts and trousers help protect you from ticks, as does insect repellent.

> ☞ **HINT: Since ticks are attracted to dark colored clothing, consider investing in camouflage, light denim, or khakis. After each walk check yourself for these microscopic critters, and if you find any, use tweezers rather than bare fingers to remove them.**

Western rattlesnakes are poisonous and make their home in the Bay Area. They like the dryer, oak woodland and chaparral regions. These creatures are not aggressive and avoid humans unless provoked. Watch where you step and don't randomly reach into the brush where they like to hibernate. Remember, most rattlesnake victims are usually provoking the snake—keep your distance; they can leap up to twelve feet!

Like snakes, scorpions sting only in self defense. They are occasionally found snugly situated under rocks or logs. While their sting is not serious, you may want to check the insides of your shoes if you take them off during a break.

Because they are hand fed or allowed to feed on human food, many wild animals in the Bay Area are looking for a hand out. Do not be swayed by cute and cuddly critters such as squirrels, raccoons, etc., which may appear tame. In fact, animals which show no fear are often the ones you especially want to avoid.

Finally, there are occasional sightings of wild boar, deer, and yes, mountain lions. Their immediate reaction is to avoid any contact with humans. Make it easy on them by alerting them to your presence. Walking in pairs is always a good idea because conversations carry. If you are alone, you may want to take up talking to yourself, or better yet, actively practice your singing voice.

☞ **HINT: Firearms on all wilderness trail are illegal!**

Restrooms - Public restrooms in San Francisco are somewhat scarce. We suggest slipping into one of the many hotels, fast food chains, or department stores in the city. Gas stations and fast food restaurants are usually a good bet when on the road. We always indicate where restroom facilities are located in the specific parks discussed in this book.

Shopping hours - Most stores in the Bay Area are open between 10:00 AM and 6:00 PM. Department stores and many specialty shops frequently offer evening hours.

Telephones - Public telephones are not difficult to find in the Bay Area. Hotels, shops, gas stations, and street corners all have them. Usually the charge is $ .20 for a local, three-minute call. If you're calling outside the immediate area, expect the operator to voice an additional charge.

> ☞ **HINT: When dialing numbers in different counties make sure you've got the right area code: (415) for San Francisco, Marin, and San Mateo counties; (408) in Santa Cruz and Santa Clara; (707) in Napa and Sonoma counties; and (510) for Alameda and Contra Costa counties. You must dial 1 before the area code as in, 1-415-555-1212. Local information is 411. To access information, dial 1, the area code, and 555-1212.**

Tipping - Sometimes an awkward dilemma, here are helpful gratuity guidelines: Porters, skycaps, doormen ($1 per bag); In restaurants (15-20% of pre-tax total); Taxi drivers (10-20% of fare); Valet parking ($1-$5).

Tourist Information Offices - Only the larger Bay Area cities provide visitor information centers. For specific information on smaller cities check in the Yellow Pages for the Chamber of Commerce.

San Francisco Visitor Information Center: (415) 391-2000; Lower level, Hallidie Plaza, 900 Market Street near the intersection of Powell and Market streets. Obtain a San Francisco information packet by writing the Convention and Visitors Bureau at P.O. Box 42907, San Francisco, CA 94142-9097.

Oakland Visitor Information Center: (510) 839-9000; Jack London Square in Downtown Oakland.

San Jose Visitor Information Center: (408) 283-8833; 333 West San Carlos Street, Suite 1000, San Jose.

Sonoma Valley Visitors Bureau: (707) 996-1090; located on the Carneros Highway (121) near the Viansa Winery.

Foreign Travelers

Customs - If you're journeying direct from other countries it is most likely you'll fly into SFO which has custom facilities to accommodate foreign visitors. Regulations vary according to the country of origin and your planned length of stay. A valid passport is required for all foreign visitors, but it's wise to check with your country's American Consul for exact details.

Foreign Currency - International visitors can exchange foreign currency or travelers' checks in SFO's central international terminal. Bank of America (branches on 345 Montgomery Street, 1 Powell Street at Hallidie Plaza, and 420 Post Street on Union Square) offers a currency exchange service, as does American Express (237 Post Street).

☞ HINT: Money hassles are alleviated when foreign visitors purchase travelers' checks in U.S. Currency rather
than their own.

Restaurants, shops, and other vendors widely accept credit
cards, particularly Mastercard, Visa, and American Express.
These make currency transactions much easier and you can also
use them to retrieve cash from bank tellers or, in certain cases,
from the ATM machines located outside most American banks.

☞ HINT: The International Visitor's Information Service provides help for those having difficulties with
English. They can help you with directions, accommodations, shopping, and medical care. French (415)
391-2003, German (415) 391-2004, Spanish (415) 391-
2122, Japanese (415) 391-2101.

Rules of the Road

Keep these ideas in mind while on the trail for your safety
and the safety of others.

1. Plan your walking route beforehand. Also make sure you
have your *Walking Easy* guidebook and a supplementary map
from park headquarters.
2. In addition to planning your route, make sure you've
brought all the necessary equipment along.
3. Check the local paper or phone for the day's weather
forecast (see timing pp. 12-13).
4. Don't pick anything along the trails—especially wildflowers. It's illegal!
5. Do not deviate from the main trail. This protects walkers from dangers such as poison oak and yellow jacket nests,
and helps combat trail erosion.
6. Proceed at your own pace, especially on more challenging
trails.

7. Trails vary from "single track" to "multipurpose." Often you are sharing the road with horses, joggers, and mountain bikers. Trail etiquette, especially on multipurpose trails open to all, dictates that pedestrians give way to horses, while bikers must give way to horses and pedestrians. Single track trails are usually narrow paths reserved for walkers and joggers only. Horses are occasionally permitted.

8. Be Prepared! Review issues under "Trail Safety" pp. 24-26.

Explanation of Symbols

Walks are designed for active adults of all ages who are in good health. Below is a guide to the *Easy Walking* symbols which appear at the beginning of each walk:

Gentle low impact walks are shorter with fewer ascents and descents and wider paths.

Comfortable walks are longer with varied terrain which may include more frequent climbing.

More challenging ascents and descents or longer trails which may be narrow and rocky.

Trail Maps are **not** drawn to scale. They are meant to provide a general idea of each walk's course. Be sure to pick up additional maps available at the respective parks.

SAN FRANCISCO

While San Francisco's population stopped growing decades ago, the city's open space is increasing dramatically. That's good news indeed for the *Easy Walker*. With staircase walks and parks all over town, this city of 750,000 is the kind of place that seems built for pedestrians. As park acreage proliferates the visitor can enjoy the coast, head inland, or enjoy a day in one of the nation's great urban refuges.

Although explorers began visiting the Pacific Coast in the 16th century, the first Spanish navigator didn't spot the Golden Gate until 1769. Six years later the Spanish vessel *San Carlos* became the first to enter San Francisco Bay. In 1776 the missionaries arrived and began colonizing the Native Americans. That same year the Spanish also created their military base at Fort Point.

While the Russians also explored these waters, San Francisco remained under Spanish and later Mexican control. Modern San Francisco is a product of the Gold Rush, an event that turned its harbor into a maritime parking lot, bringing the wild west in with a big bang as vigilantes made a mockery of law and order.

As this emerging metropolis started to gentrify, civic leaders began fashioning a preservationist spirit that makes San Francisco a world favorite among knowledgeable travelers. The Gold Rush and statehood in 1850 created a boom that brought in settlers from around the world. The West's first real melting pot, San Francisco also attracted a new breed of urban planners and pioneer conservationists determined to preserve the city's unique assets.

As you explore the city today it seems like every other block is either a landmark or a civic monument. From Jack Kerouac Street to Sutro Garden, San Francisco is the legacy of people who succumbed to its charms and were determined to hand them on to future generations. It's no accident that the *San Francisco Chronicle*'s Herb Caen has been writing a daily column longer than anyone else in America—56 years. The narcissistic locals never tire of Caen's favorite topic, the city by the bay.

To appreciate what captures and captivates the millions who visit this city each year, it's necessary to go beyond the downtown towers and explore some of the neighborhoods that are the focus of the walks in this section. The Marina, Golden Gate Park, the Richmond, the Presidio, these are just a few of the places that illustrate the city's diversity.

While the region's first inhabitants, the Ohlone and Miwok Indians who once had this region to themselves, were devastated by white man's diseases, it is still possible to learn their history at places like the Oakland Museum (see East Bay Chapter). Books such as Malcolm Margolin's *The Ohlone Way* (Heyday Books) also help recreate this pre-European era when perhaps 30 or 40 Ohlone villages were found along the San Francisco Bay.

"The Ohlones" Margolin writes, "lived in an unchanging world, a world they knew so intimately that even individual rocks, trees, and clumps of bushes had names." By contrast the white settlers created a new San Francisco, a city that refused to stand still for a moment.

A new generation of entrepreneurs, men with names like Stanford, Crocker, Hopkins, and Huntington took their spoils from the Gold Rush boom and went to work on a transcontinental railroad. George Hearst, another mining king, gave his son Will the money to found a newspaper empire memorialized in the film classic *Citizen Kane*. And a cable maker named Andrew Hallidie pioneered a new transportation system for the city that would replace the horse drawn coach.

Only the great San Francisco earthquake of 1906 seemed able to temper the restlessness of this city's master builders. In the aftermath of this great disaster, leaders began to fully realize the value of green space like Golden Gate Park, a major refuge for the newly homeless.

Much of the region you are about to explore has been spared from the bulldozer and the construction crane by the work of a dedicated crew of preservationists working closely with state and national politicians who knew a good thing when they saw it. Perhaps the most important part of this greenbelt is the 144,000-acre Golden Gate National Recreation Area.

Conceived in 1962 after the federal prison on Alcatraz was closed, it was modeled after the East Coast's Gateway National Recreation Area. With the support of conservation groups like the Sierra Club and the Audubon Society, organizers persuaded Congress to create this new preserve. President Kennedy signed the park bill in 1962 and it was dedicated four years later by Ladybird Johnson. In 1983 the GGNRA was dedicated to Congressman Phillip Burton, a key political figure behind the creation of this preserve.

Key units included the Aquatic Park area at the north end of Fisherman's Wharf, Fort Mason Center, the Marina Green, Golden Gate Promenade and Fort Point. Sweeping from Hyde Street Pier on the city's north end to Fort Funston south of Ocean Beach, this portion of the recreation area creates a beautiful oceanfront path you'll want to explore.

While Golden Gate Park is San Francisco's leading refuge, the city has also created many pocket parks dotting areas like Pacific Heights and Presidio Heights. Some offer grand Bay views while others are major community hubs. North Beach's Washington Park, Russian Hill Park, and Chinatown's Portsmouth Square are also great community gathering places. Perhaps the most incongruous park in town is the redwood grove located behind the city's tallest building, the Transamerica Pyramid.

While other cities watch prime parkland fall to developers, San Francisco preservationists continue to win round after round. The 90s have been a particularly heady period as the vast Presidio landscape on the city's northwest site has been given to the city by the U.S. Army. Like a second Golden Gate Park, this treasure adds to the legacy of San Franciscans determined to keep their city just the way it came.

The Feel of Walks in San Francisco

San Francisco walks detailed here avoid urban haunts and are primarily located in parklands and semi-wilderness areas. All are gentle, often rimming the shoreline while incorporating other popular San Francisco sights. Much of the rugged terrain and vegetation—rocky cliffs, and sculptured cypress trees—put you in touch with the region's past. Dress warmly as strong winds often ventilate the coast.

How to get to San Francisco

Before the 1930s there was only one entry portal into the city, the Ferry Building. Today tens of thousands commute into the city daily via the Golden Gate Bridge from the North Bay and the Bay Bridge from the east. For those heading north to San Francisco from the peninsula, several highways (I-280, U.S. 101) feed into the city.

Sights and Excursions in San Francisco

South of Market

You say you are hungry for cappuccino and culture. You think you can go another night without a nightclub featuring a swimming pool that turns into a dance floor. You hunger for design centers and a funky side of San Francisco that the Grey Line passes by as quickly as possible. Well good for you. You're definitely ready for South of Market ("SoMa").

1. Yerba Buena Center for the Arts. (415) 978-2787. The focal point of the new arts district budding South of Market, the Yerba Buena Center houses several galleries, a theater, and cafe. Arts classes are offered and events are staged inside and outdoors in the garden park.
Directions: Bounded by Third, Fourth, Mission, and Folsom streets.

2. San Francisco Museum of Modern Art. (Open 11-6 daily; (415) 357-4000.) Just moved from its former location on Van Ness to a new South of Market facility, this museum is now large enough to display additional pieces from its personal collection, including the likes of Picasso, Matisse, Klee,

O'Keeffe, Kandinsky, Rivera, and Pollock. Designed by Swiss Architect Mario Botta, this 250,000 square-foot structure has a stylish interior with skylights, high ceilings, and a smooth black granite surface, tastefully complementing exhibits of American and European modern art, architecture, design, and 20th-century photography.

Directions: The San Francisco Museum of Modern Art is located at 151 3rd Street between Mission and Howard streets.

3. Ansel Adams Center. (Open 11 to 5 Tuesday through Sunday; (415) 495-7000.) Hosting the West Coast's largest repository of photographic art, the Ansel Adams Center features five galleries: four host changing exhibits featuring works of photographers past and present, and one exclusively displays the work of nature photographer Ansel Adams.

Directions: 250 Fourth Street, between Howard and Folsom streets.

Civic Center

Designed by architect Daniel Burnham, this San Francisco hub is the middleground between frenzied downtown and quieter residential districts. Centered around domed City Hall, this area includes the Veterans Building, the Civic Auditorium, Louise M. Davies Symphony Hall, and the War Memorial Opera House. In the neighborhood are state and federal office buildings, fine restaurants, and the popular Opera Plaza shopping complex.

4. City Hall. A 1915 Beaux Arts structure designed by Arthur Brown (designer of the War Memorial Opera House, Berkeley's City Hall, and Coit Tower) and John Bakewell Jr. as part of San Francisco's "City Beautiful" movement. A mini version of the nation's capitol, the Dome is modeled after Saint Peter's in the Vatican. Sculptures grace the entrances. This building is also the site of one of the city's great tragedies. In 1978 former San Francisco Supervisor Dan White shot and killed Mayor George Moscone and Supervisor Harvey Milk here.

Directions: Located in the Civic Center area bounded by Polk, Grove, Van Ness and McAllister streets.

In addition to City Hall the area boasts several other note-worthy structures. **Louis B. Davies Symphony Hall** (210 Van Ness, at Grove; (415) 431-5400), named after the San Francisco philanthropist, is the contemporary home of the San Francisco Symphony.

The **War Memorial Opera House** (301 Van Ness Avenue, at Grove; (415) 864-6000) is a grand, 1930s structure where San Francisco's opera and ballet companies perform.

The **Veterans Building** (401 Van Ness, at McAllister) is another Brown and Bakewell building and former home to the San Francisco Museum of Modern Art. Today it houses the Herbst Theater concert and lecture hall.

Financial District

Wall Street West, the Financial District is Northern Calif-ornia's commercial center. A hub for Pacific Rim trade, home of major banks, and the Pacific Stock Exchange, this district is close to the city's primary shopping area and convenient to leading hotels and restaurants.

> ☞ **HINT: Justin Herman Plaza, at the foot of Market Street, is the Financial District's best place to lunch. Chose from one of the many different eateries, sit by Vaillancourt Fountain, enjoy midday entertainment weekdays, and watch hoards of business executives refuel.**

The original entrance to San Francisco for North and East Bay commuters before construction of the Golden Gate and Bay bridges, the **Ferry Building** was constructed in 1896. Based on the Cathedral Tower of Seville, this landmark is now the home of the World Trade Center.

The 48-story **Transamerica Pyramid** (600 Montgomery, at Washington), at 853 feet, has been the tallest building in the city since 1977. The 27th floor is open to the public.

Rivaling the pyramid is the **Bank of America Building** (555 California Street). Visitors often enjoy popping up to the

Carnelian Room on the 52nd floor for evening drinks and Sunday brunch. The black sculpture outside the building is nicknamed "Banker's Heart."

Nob Hill

Nob Hill, located at the summit of California Street, came alive with the Gold Rush. Nearly 150 years later it remains one of the city's magical places. The mining barons chose this scenic spot as the perfect location for their castles and villas. Today several of San Francisco's leading hotels are found here and it's a great place to round out a day of *Easy Walking*.

At the top you'll find pure luxury at the **Fairmont** (950 Mason Street, between California and Sacramento), **Mark Hopkins** (California and Mason streets), **Stanford Court** (at California and Powell), and **Huntington** (California and Taylor) hotels. The setting for television's long running series, "Hotel," the Fairmont is as spectacular in real life as it is on screen.

In the center of it all rests quaint, two-acre Huntington Park with a small playground for children and, next door, the prestigious, all-male Pacific Union Club.

> ☞ **HINT: Top of the Mark, located at the summit of the Mark Hopkins Hotel, is one of the city's most popular watering holes. Drinks are expensive, but the view is magnificent.**

5. Grace Cathedral. A showplace for the Protestant elite, Grace Cathedral is a magnificent amalgam of beautiful structures around the world. Its doors are famous casts from the molds of Ghiberti's "Gates of Paradise" gracing the Baptistry in Florence. The lovely, stained-glass, rose window was inspired by Paris's Notre Dame. Inside you'll find a 13th-century Catalonian crucifix, 15th-century Flemish altar, and 16th-century Gobelin tapestry from Brussels.

Directions: The Cathedral is located at 1051 Taylor Street between California and Sacramento streets.

☞ **HINT: If your visit to San Francisco occurs during the holiday season, try and fit a Pipe Organ concert or choral event at Grace Cathedral into your schedule.**

6. San Francisco Cable Car Museum. (Open 10 to 6 summer months and 10 to 5 winter months; (415) 474-1887.) Situated in a 1907 three-tiered brick structure, the museum displays machinery, Andrew Hallidie's original car design, and includes a short video on the inner workings of these classic cars.

Directions: Located on Washington and Mason streets in the Nob Hill district.

Chinatown

Brought to this state in the mid-nineteenth century as virtual indentured servants, the Chinese played a crucial role in the building of California. Today their descendants are front and center in every aspect of city life. Chinatown is now one of San Francisco's cultural landmarks, a place where many of the city's 140,000 Chinese live. This district is centered around Grant Avenue, the oldest street in San Francisco.

7. Chinatown Gate. Modeled after the many ceremonial gates in Chinese villages, the Chinatown Gate (at Grant and Bush) is a fitting place to begin a tour of this historical neighborhood.

8. The Chinese Historical Society of America. (Open Noon to 4 Tuesday through Saturday; (415) 391-1188.) This is the only museum in the U.S. to catalog through exhibits, artifacts, and photographs, Chinese American History. A gift shop is on site and monthly meetings are open to the public.

Directions: Located at 650 Commercial Street between Kearny and Montgomery streets.

9. Chinese Culture Center. (Open 9 to 5:30 Tuesday through Saturday; (415) 986-1822.) The Chinese Culture Center hosts rotating exhibits, featuring historical and contemporary Chinese arts. The center organizes community events, walking tours of the neighborhood, and can answer any questions you may have about the Chinese-American community.

Directions: Located on the third floor of the Chinatown Holiday Inn at 750 Kearny Street.

North Beach

Eager to expand the city's boundaries, civic leaders filled in this waterfront area more than a century ago. While the turf may be manmade, there's nothing artificial about this largely Italian neighborhood that is big on nightlife, restaurants, and coffeehouses. The birthplace of the beat scene, a cultural hub, and the easiest way to reach Telegraph Hill's Coit Tower, North Beach is a must for any *Easy Walker*. Come walk in the shadow of Kerouac, Ginsburg, and Ferlinghetti.

10. City Lights Bookstore. (Open 10 AM TO 11:45 PM; (415) 362-8193.) A San Francisco landmark since 1953, City Lights is owned and operated by Beat Poet Lawrence Ferlinghetti. The maze-like interior serves as a literary meeting place and boasts a wide selection of poetry, avant-garde and, of course, Beat literature.

Directions: 261 Columbus Avenue, on the corner of Jack Kerouac Street.

11. Washington Square Park. An encampment for homeless victims after the 1906 earthquake that devastated North Beach, the square is now a wonderful place to relax on a sunny morning or afternoon, eating pastries from one of the many Italian bakeries, and eavesdropping on nearby conversations.

Directions: Bounded by Union, Filbert, and Stockton streets and Columbus Avenue in the center of North Beach.

12. Saint Peter & Paul Catholic Church. The "Italian Cathedral" of San Francisco, this Gothic Revival structure was completed in 1924. Sunday masses are celebrated in English, Italian, and Chinese, and twin spires, rising 191 feet, grace the facade.

Directions: 666 Filbert Street on the north side of Washington Square.

13. Coit Tower. This 180-foot phallic structure, built in 1934, was financed by and named after Lillie Hitchcock Coit, an eccentric San Francisco socialite with a passion for firemen. Many believe the tower design was modeled after a fire hose nozzle. Housed inside are WPA murals depicting California laborers. From the top, spectacular views of Alcatraz, Angel Island, Mount Tamalpais, and the shores of Berkeley and Oakland extend across the Bay

Directions: Located at the top of Telegraph Hill Boulevard.

Fisherman's Wharf

It's hard to find fishermen at Fisherman's Wharf. You will find restaurants, lots of them, along with shops and museums, souvenir stands, hotels, historic ships, street artists, and ferry terminals that can whisk you out to Alcatraz or Angel Island.

This popular destination, located at the end of the cable car line is the very essence of San Francisco rubbernecking. As much a part of San Francisco as the Golden Gate Bridge, Fisherman's Wharf is the kind of place where the sourdough bread is always fresh and the shrimp in your cocktail may have just come in off the truck from Oregon.

14. Pier 39. Pier 39 is considered to be San Francisco's number one tourist destination. Even if you don't like crowds, you may want to visit the **sea lions** which have one-upped the Pier's tourist kitsch. When these marine mammals arrived at the sailboat docks in 1989, tourism increased dramatically. The boats were moved out and now the sea lions have their own mini-sanctuary.

The pier is also a good place for a general introduction to the historical sights and sounds of this great city. **The San Francisco Experience** (located on the second level of Pier 39; (415) 388-6032) features a surround-sound, cinematic vision of San Francisco's past and present including the Gold Rush, cable cars, the Golden Gate Bridge, and some of the city's famed neighborhoods.

Directions: Pier 39 is located on the Embarcadero near Beach Street.

15. Alcatraz. The infamous maximum security prison established in 1934, "The Rock" was home to Al Capone, "Machine Gun" Kelly, and Robert "Birdman of Alcatraz" Stroud. The prison was shut down in 1963 and occupied in 1969 for two years by Native Americans trying to reclaim their rightful land. The island is now preserved and managed by the Golden Gate National Recreation Area. Tours are hosted daily. A visit to Alcatraz is a unique and fascinating experience.

Directions: Access to Alcatraz is by ferry only. The Red and White Ferry offers service from pier 41. Phone (415) 546-2700 for details.

16. Aquatic Park. This waterfront park filled with street vendors and budding musicians is also the site of **Hyde Street Pier** and the **San Francisco National Maritime Museum** (Open 10 to 5 daily; (415) 556-3002).

Anchored at Hyde Street Pier are six historic ships: the *Alma*, a 1891 Scow Schooner; *C.A. Thayer*, an 1895 coastal cargo ship; respective paddle and tug boats, *Eppleton Hall* (1914) and *Hercules* (1907); the *Eureka*, an 1890s Bay Area commuter ferry; and the pride of the fleet, the *Balclutha*, a Scottish 1886 square-rigged sailing ship that's been around Cape Horn 17 times.

The San Francisco Maritime Museum (Beach and Polk streets) was originally built to house a casino, but the art deco, ship-like structure makes a perfect museum. Surveying San Francisco's maritime history, the museum exhibits models, ship artifacts, maps, and photography.

Directions: Located on Beach Street at the waterfront between Hyde Street and Van Ness.

17. Exploratorium. (Open 10 to 5 Tuesday through Sunday; (415) 561-0360.) A museum of science emphasizing human perception, the Exploratorium showcases over 700 exhibits. Many are hands-on displays designed to educate and entertain.

Directions: 3601 Lyon Street between Marina Boulevard and Lombard Street at the Palace of Fine Arts. Via public transportation take the #30 bus from the Montgomery Street BART station.

The Presidio

Set on more than 1,500 acres of prime San Francisco real estate, the Presidio has functioned as a Military Base since the Spanish invasion in 1776. Once a rocky, rugged coastline, the Presidio's parklike ambiance is the result of extensive planting and landscaping over the past century. Now that the Army has closed its base here, the land is being administered by the GGNRA, much to the envy of ambitious developers.

Directions: The Presidio's main entrance is located at Lombard and Lyon streets.

18. The Presidio Museum. (Open 10 to 4 Wednesday through Sunday; (415) 556-0856.) Focusing on San Francisco's military history back to 1776, the Presidio Museum is located in the circa 1860 Old Station Hospital. After you've had a chance to see the military uniforms and weapon collections, wander the nearby grounds. Information on several short hikes within the Presidio is available at the museum.

Directions: Located at Lincoln Boulevard and Funston Avenue within the Presidio.

19. California Palace of the Legion of Honor. (415) 863-3330. Scheduled to reopen in November 1995, the Palace of the Legion of Honor has been undergoing seismic restructuring and expansion. Forty-two percent more space will be allotted to displaying its treasures.

The inspiration of Alma deBretteville Spreckels, a San Francisco socialite who wanted a spectacular place to harbor French art, this is a palace indeed, featuring an extensive collection of

French and European artists. Gracing the exterior courtyard is Rodin's "The Thinker," one of five original castings.

Directions: Located in Lincoln Park. Head west on Geary and make a right on 34th Avenue until you reach Clement.

20. California Academy of Sciences. (Open 10 to 5 daily; (415) 750-7145.) Housing **Morrison Planetarium**, **Steinhart Aquarium**, and the **Natural History Museum**, the California Academy of Sciences is the place for budding biologists, shark enthusiasts, astronomy buffs, and devotees of California wildlife.

Sky shows and Laserium light shows are featured at the Planetarium. The Aquarium is North America's oldest with a Fish Roundabout hosting over 14,000 different sea creatures and a living coral reef tank.

Within the Natural History Museum check out the Gem and Mineral Hall and the African Hall's lion and zebra dioramas. Comic strip aficionados will love the Far Side Science Gallery displaying 160 cartoons by Gary Larson. Experience this State's diverse habitats in "Wild California" or learn about the origin of the species in "Life Through Time."

Directions: Located on the Music Concourse in Golden Gate Park. If you're using public transport, take the #38 bus from Union Square to 6th Street and Geary, then transfer onto the #44 bus to the park.

> ☞ **HINT: Many San Francisco Museums offer discounts on entrance admission if you use public transportation and present a fast pass or transfer stub.**

21. M.H. De Young Memorial Museum. (Open 10 to 5 Thursday through Sunday; (415) 863-3330.) Founded in 1894 as a city museum with insignificant art, the de Young is now known for an extensive permanent collection of art from the United States and the Americas (Mesoamerica, Central, and South America).

Housed in 22 galleries, the collection ranges from the Colonial era to the mid-twentieth century. African art, impressive textiles, and decorative arts and crafts are also shown. Artists permanently featured include Bingham, Cassat, Copley, Homer, and Whistler. Exhibitions displaying European artists are hosted regularly and add a touch of variety to the American theme.

Directions: See directions for the California Academy of Sciences above.

> ☞ **HINT: For a great deal, visit the Exploratorium, California Academy of Sciences, the de Young Memorial, and Asian Art museums on the first Wednesday of every month when they offer free admission.**

22. Asian Art Museum. (Adjoining the de Young Museum; (415) 668-8921.) The Asian Art Museum opened in 1966 as the permanent site of Avery Brundage's impressive art collection. Today it is the West's largest exhibition of Asian Art. Over 500 pieces are featured on the main floor as part of the museum's permanent Chinese collection.

Floors and galleries are partitioned to display art from Korea, India, Tibet, Nepal, Pakistan, Japan, and Southeast Asia. Visiting exhibitions are just as spectacular—the museum recently displayed Xi'an's terracotta warriors in "Tomb Treasures from China: The Buried Art of Ancient Xi'an."

> ☞ **HINT: The entrance fee to either the de Young or Asian Art museums automatically includes same day admission to the other.**

23. Stern Grove Summer Concert Series. (415) 252-6252. In the idyllic setting of Stern Grove, you can enjoy quality opera, symphonies, jazz, musicals, and ballet. The nation's oldest continual summer concert series is still free, and definitely one of the best places to picnic and relax on a summer Sunday afternoon. Bring a blanket or warm jacket, as late afternoons can get chilly when the fog starts rolling in. Highly recommended.

Directions: Stern Grove is located at Sloat Boulevard and 19th Avenue.

24. San Francisco Zoo. (Open 10 to 5 daily; (415) 753-7083.) Located at Sloat Boulevard and the Great Highway, the San Francisco Zoo is the place to see Sumatran tigers, greater one-horned rhinos, a rain forest aviary, and a Big Cat house.

Highlights include the Primate Discovery Center, Koala Crossing, and Gorilla World. There's also a popular children's petting zoo. The zoo is also next door to Lake Merced where you can fish for trout or rent small boats.

Directions: Located at Sloat Boulevard and 45th Avenue.

Shopping

San Francisco is a shopper's dream. Check out the discount outlets South of Market, or the Financial District's Embarcadero Center with its three-tier, maze-like pedestrian mall. Pier 39 is good for deals on tourist collectibles, while the nearby Ghiradelli Square and Cannery, both converted warehouses, offer unique shops and eateries.

Large department stores and chic boutiques surround Union Square, and the San Francisco Shopping Center at Market and Powell streets, with a circular escalator leading up to Nordstroms, is a delightful taste of opulence.

San Francisco's shopping hub is Union Square. While many of the great stores like Magnin's and the City of Paris are gone, it's still possible to enjoy the sophisticated ambiance of this downtown shopping mecca. Among the major stores you'll find here are Macy's, Gumps, Sak's Fifth Avenue, Bullock and Jones.

Just off Union Square's east side is Maiden Lane where you'll find impressionist prints at the Richard Thompson Gallery (#80) and fine designer jewelry, paintings, and graphics at the rotunda shaped Circle Gallery (#140).

When you need a break, head over to the Neiman Marcus Rotunda restaurant (open daily, 2:30 to 5; (415) 363-4777) or the St. Francis Hotel Compass Rose (open daily, 3 to 5; (415) 397-7000) for high tea.

Accommodations

The Archbishops Mansion - 1000 Fulton Street; (415) 563-7872 [$115-285]. A Grand structure dating back to 1904, The Archbishops Mansion was, yes, built for the Archbishop. Its guest and sitting rooms are warm and spectacularly furnished with fireplaces, period antiques, embroidered linens, and even a 1904 Bechstein grand piano previously owned by Noel Coward. A continental breakfast is served daily and guests are also welcome to enjoy the complimentary afternoon wine service in the French Parlor each afternoon. [Proprietors: Jeffery Ross and Jonathan Shannon]

The Bed and Breakfast Inn - Four Charlton Court, in San Francisco, off Union Street; (415) 921-9784 [$70-225]. Four Charlton Court is a ten-room haven just a step away from the bustling city. Guests may chose from four "pension"-style rooms with shared facilities or six additional deluxe accommodations, all including a continental breakfast served each morning. Lovely antiques add to the country inn atmosphere where guests are pampered and encouraged to make use of the library and gardens. [Proprietors: Robert and Marily Kavanaugh]

Cornell Hotel - 715 Bush Street, downtown San Francisco; (415) 421-3154, fax (415) 399-1442, [$60-95]. Authentic French charm defines this 60-room hostelry conveniently located between Union Square and Nob Hill. Sitting atop the quaint Jeanne D'Arc restaurant, decorated with tapestries and Medieval artifacts, guests can also arrange a special week-long package which includes breakfast each morning and dinner for five nights.

The Majestic - 1500 Sutter Street, San Francisco off Gough Street; (415) 441-1100, fax (415) 673-7331 [$125-250]. Sixty luxurious rooms and lavish suites with all the amenities of a deluxe rate hotel, including a gourmet restaurant and classy bar, are featured at The Majestic. Guests are treated warmly, and bedrooms in this beautiful Edwardian structure are large and comfortably decorated in soft hues graced with period French and English antiques. Luxury without a luxury tariff.

Petite Auberge - 863 Bush Street, just four blocks from Union Square; (415) 928-6000, fax (415) 775-5717 [$110-220]. Twenty-six charming rooms grace this petite romantic inn which follows its French county theme all the way from quaint lace curtains and terracotta tiles, to a country market mural decorating the dining room. A full breakfast is served each morning as are complementary wine and munchies in the afternoon. [Proprietor: Celeste Lytle]

The Queen Anne Hotel - 1590 Sutter Street, at Octavia in Lower Pacific Heights; (415) 441-2828; fax (415) 775-5212 [$99-275]. Forty-nine guest rooms and suites grace this fully restored, 1890s Queen Anne. Amenities include a morning paper served with your continental breakfast, limousine service to downtown, access to health facilities, and complimentary tea and sherry in the evenings. In addition to friendly, personal service, rooms are warmly furnished with Victorian pieces and most have bay windows and fireplaces.

The Spencer House - 1080 Haight Street, in the Haight-Ashbury district; (415) 626-9205, fax (415) 626-9208, [$95-155]. A prime locale in the funky Haight neighborhood, this treasure is a mere six blocks away from Golden Gate Park. Enjoy the modern day boutiques and nearby eateries then step back in time as you cross the Spenser House threshold. You are welcomed with complimentary port or sherry in a private room richly decorated with antique furnishings and fixtures, and the next morning, a gourmet breakfast to dream about. [Innkeepers: Barbara and Jack Chambers]

The Washington Square Inn - 1660 Stockton Street in North Beach; (415) 981-4220, fax (415) 397-7242 [$85-180]. This small hotel offers the personal comfort of a Bed and Breakfast plus a few additional perks such as valet parking, daily paper delivery to your door, and polished shoes each morning. Rooms are tastefully decorated with French and English antiques, and the North Beach locale makes this cozy enclave a delight for *Easy Walkers*. [Proprietors: Nan and Norm Rosenblatt]

Restaurants

Bix Restaurant and Lounge - 56 Gold Street, located in between the Financial District and North Beach; (415) 433-6300. Step into Bix, and enter the dark intriguing atmosphere of a 1940s supper club. The seafood and meat dishes won't disappoint in this lively yet formal restaurant. Live music. Expensive. Reservations required.

Boudin Sourdough Bakery & Cafe - The original baker of San Francisco sourdough French bread, Boudin has bakeries all over the city that can set *Easy Walkers* up with sandwiches to go. Check the Yellow Pages for the location closest to you.

Bucci Cafe - 478 Green Street, in North Beach; (415) 981-2044. While Bucci's isn't much from the outside, diners are pleasantly surprised when they walk through the lushly planted alleyway leading to this comfortable restaurant. The bar is the hub of a major singles scene and there's a cozy outdoor garden. The tasty Italian fare is excellent and inexpensive. Arrive early or reserve in advance. There is often a long wait at this one.

Buena Vista Cafe - 2765 Hyde Street, near Aquatic Park; (415) 474-5044. This popular corner restaurant and bar serves inexpensive sandwiches and burgers and makes the best Irish Coffees in San Francisco. Close to Ghiradelli Square and The Cannery, the Buena Vista Cafe is a convenient place to rest between shopping and sightseeing. The bar is often crowded.

Cafe Bastille - 22 Belden Place, between Pine, Bush, Kearny, and Montgomery streets in the Financial District; (415) 986-5673. Enjoy fine, moderately-priced, French cuisine in this lively restaurant with a relaxed atmosphere. The crepes are out of this world and if you visit on a Thursday or Friday evening you'll enjoy live jazz with your meal. Service is friendly. Reservations recommended.

California Culinary Academy - California Hall, 625 Polk Street, near the Civic Center; (415) 771-3500. Two restaurants are featured at the Culinary Academy: The Academy Grill, specializing in American fare, and the main Careme Room, serving international cuisine with a contemporary edge. The grill is informal while the Careme Room is a bit more upscale. All meals are prepared by students supervised by a skillful faculty. When the food is excellent, as it often is, you're getting a great deal. Open Monday through Friday only.

Fog City Diner - 1300 Battery Street in the Financial District; (415) 982-2000. Bright neon lights and a curvy, chrome, art deco exterior make Fog City Diner hard to miss. This "upscale" diner boasts an oyster bar, serves American classics, and more. Moderately priced. Reservations recommended.

Greens at Fort Mason - Building A in the Marina District's Fort Mason Center; (415) 771-6222. Haute vegetarian cuisine, Greens has been a Bay Area favorite since it opened in 1979. Enjoy wonderful views of the Golden Gate while dining on innovative entrees that redefine the concept of vegetarian cuisine. Operated by San Francisco's Zen Center. Reservations required.

Hayes Street Grill - 320 Hayes Street; (415) 863-5545. Within walking distance of Civic Center sights, this is the place to go for fresh fish prepared simply and perfectly. Grilled, sautéed, or steamed, diners decide how they want their meal prepared and also select their own sauce. Afterwards indulge in the always excellent creme brulee. Pleasant dining room atmosphere. Moderately priced. Reservations recommended.

Kuleto's - 221 Powell Street near Geary Street off Union Square; (415) 397-7720. Contemporary Italian dining in a lively, convivial environment. Quality cuisine, generous portions, and friendly service make Kuleto's an enjoyable, moderately-priced eatery. Reservations recommended.

MacArthur Park - 607 Front Street on Jackson Square; (415) 398-5700. A moderately priced restaurant serving American fare and specializing in oakwood-smoked, baby back ribs and fresh mesquite-grilled fresh fish. Wicker, ficus trees, track lighting, and exposed brick walls add to the chic, yet casual atmosphere. Reservations recommended.

Mario's Bohemian Cigar Store and Cafe - 566 Columbus Avenue at Union Street in North Beach; (415) 362-0536.

A cafe, bar, and restaurant all in one, Mario's doesn't sell cigars but serves, in addition to standard cafe fare, delicious sandwiches prepared with focaccia. Overlooks Washington Square. No reservations required.

Molinari Delicatessen - 373 Columbus Avenue; (415) 421-2337. Housing an overwhelming selection of gourmet eats, you'll have lots of fun here creating your picnic for the day.

Natoma Cafe - 145 Natoma Street, south of Market near the Moscone Center; (415) 495-3289. Whips up specialty sandwiches and salads.

One Market - 1 Market Street, on the Embarcadero; (415) 777-5577. Occupying the historic 1917 Southern Pacific Building, One Market serves California cuisine prepared in a wood burning oven. All breads and deserts are made fresh on the premises. An impressive American wine list. Evening jazz pianist adds to the ambiance. Reservations required.

Postrio - 545 Post Street, just off Union Square; (415) 776-7825. One of Wolfgang Puck's northern offspring, this restaurant's spacious dinning room makes for an exciting dinning experience. Exceptional dishes include roasted salmon and almond black pepper crust served on a warm spinach salad with balsamic vinegar. Beautifully furnished—wild decor. Expensive. Reservations recommended.

The Ramp - 855 China Basin Street, in South Beach; (415) 621-2378. Casual and inexpensive, The Ramp is an eclectic spot decorated with mismatched tables and chairs. On warm summer afternoons it's a pleasure to sit on the outdoor patio overlooking the Bay. In the evenings The Ramp converts to a bar with live Jazz and Latin tunes.

Square One - 190 Pacific Avenue at Front Street in the Financial District; (415) 788-1110. Excellent Mediterranean dishes from Italy, Portugal, France, North Africa, and elsewhere. Each entree is prepared California style, with the freshest ingredients, and the deluxe menu changes daily. Simple, elegant decor. Reservations required.

Stars - 150 Redwood Alley, off Van ness between McAllister Street and Golden Gate Avenue, near the Civic Center; (415) 861-7827. Expect to spend a lot of money for dining at its finest in this convivial and classy brasserie—the creation of superchef and owner Jeremiah Tower. Excellent seafood, pasta dishes, and delectable deserts are prepared to perfection. A lively, eclectic crowd makes for fun people watching while dining. Reservations required.

For quality without the pretense, the budget conscious traveler may want to splurge on its sibling, **Stars Cafe** (nearby at 500 Van Ness Avenue; (415) 861-4344).

The Stinking Rose - 325 Columbus Avenue, between Broadway and Vallejo streets in North Beach; (415) 781-ROSE. An upbeat restaurant with the credo: "We season our garlic with food." Here you can munch on pasta and meat dishes seeped in garlic. Those who prefer to do without can order the "vampire fare." Reservations required.

Tadich Grill - 240 California Street, below Battery in the Financial District; (415) 391-2373. Fish!!! Always fresh and at moderate prices. This established San Francisco eatery started out as a coffee salon in 1849. In 1912 it became Tadich Grill and has been pleasing diners ever since. A popular specialty is the seafood plate with oysters, prawns, scallops, and calamari.

Zuni Cafe - 1658 Market Street, between Haight and Page streets; (415) 552-2522. Simple dishes, changing daily to ensure freshness, are prepared to perfection at this super chic, yet comfortable restaurant. Try the roasted chicken with warm bread salad prepared for two. Oysters on the half shell are also a favorite starter here. If you have to wait, spend some time at the funky copper-topped bar. Reservations are not required but recommended.

San Francisco Walks

Walk #1: The Golden Gate Promenade from Fort Mason to Fort Point

Walking Easy Time
3 hours

A gentle waterfront stroll towards the Golden Gate, today's walk between Fort Mason and Fort Point conveniently incorporates visits to some of San Francisco's most popular post-military sights with panoramic views of Alcatraz and Angel Island anchored in the Bay and the awesome Marin County wilderness beyond.

Directions: Park in the Fort Mason Center parking lot located at the intersection of Marina Boulevard and Beach Street in the Marina District, just across from the Safeway supermarket.

Whether you decide to explore Fort Mason at the beginning or end of today's walk along the Promenade, consider scheduling lunch there. The Great Meadow, flanking Fort Mason on the west, is perfect for picnics.

While the GGNRA has successfully transformed surplus federal lands into a public park system, working jointly with the community Fort Mason plays a different role. Community gardens, museums, theaters, non-profit organizations, live radio shows, and restaurants have replaced the military. Located atop San Francisco's northernmost promontory, the Fort was built during the Spanish era. Black Point Battery, a relic of the Civil War era, sits just below the promontory. The piers extending into the Bay from Fort Mason Center served as the military's main embarkation port between 1910 and 1963.

Nestled between many of the buildings now serving as GGNRA Headquarters, are garden plots cultivated by community members, as well as an international youth hostel harboring young travelers from around the world.

The Great Meadow, that expanse of grass sloping west, served as a refuge center for the homeless after the devastating 1906 earthquake. Anchored at Pier Three is the last of the Liberty ships, the fully restored *Jeremiah O'Brien*, recently back from its European journey celebrating the fiftieth anniversary of D-Day.

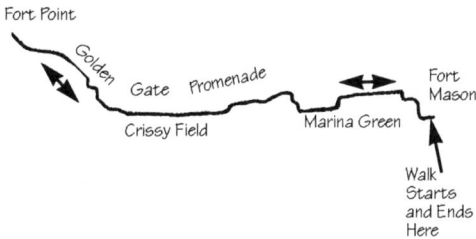

S t a r t : Bridging Fort Mason and the Presidio's Crissy Field is Marina Green, where today's walk begins. *Easy Walkers* have a choice of several pedestrian paths that rim a grass playing field and border the prestigious Saint Francis Yacht Club. Hike along San Francisco's northern shore, via the Marina Boulevard pedestrian sidewalk or tread across the grassy field. A popular site for kite flying, strong Bay breezes animate a host of colorful flying contraptions that dazzle passersby of all ages.

We recommend following the paved pathway bordering the Bay rather than the Boulevard. The kites remain visible from this vantage point and you'll have a better view of the Bay front. Don't miss the wave organ at the end of the outer sea wall extending from the Saint Francis Yacht Club. Submerged pipes at the tip create sonorous sounds when the tide is right. You may want to picnic here to the music of the swells.

After passing the field adjacent to the yacht club, veer left, away from the waterfront. At Marina Boulevard head right and, after 50 yards, right again, toward the Bay. Along this stretch, paralleling the Boulevard, note the Mediterranean-style homes dating back to the 1915 Panama Pacific International Exposition. Also here is the area's anomalous centerpiece, the Palace of Fine Arts. Designed by Bernard Maybeck for the festival, this is just one of many lavish structures that graced 635 acres in the Marina District. An object of beauty and hope, constructed only nine years after the disastrous 1906 earthquake, the Palace of Fine Arts was preserved and restored as a proud monument to that distinguished moment in San Francisco history.

Hit the shoreline once more and head left at the sign reading "San Francisco Bay Trail." Entering the northern section of the Presidio, this pathway leads to Fort Point via Crissy Field. A historic military airfield constructed in the 1920s before there even was a United States Airforce, this stretch of land was originally covered with sand dunes and salt marshes. Today portions of the field are restricted. Indigenous grasses have been planted to restore native vegetation more suited to the rugged conditions here. Rest anywhere along the field and watch windsurfers challenge amazing winds.

A parcourse with exercise stations parallels your walk through the Presidio. This is a perfect opportunity to add toning to your walking workout before reaching the fishing pier at the west end of the field. Veer left around the buildings blocking the pathway and continue another quarter mile to Fort Point. This awesome, 1861 red brick fortress stands in the shadow of the Golden Gate.

Visitors are free to tour the four-tiered National Historic Site at their leisure or join one of the scheduled tours led by knowledgeable rangers dressed in Civil War attire. Built to safeguard the city, the Fort saw little military action. Nonetheless it remained active through World War II when its brick casemates could no longer withstand modern weaponry. You may ascend the spiral staircase where, from the forth tier, you can enjoy more magnificent views of the bridge. Before leaving, be sure to purchase a souvenir from Sutler's store which dates back to the Civil War.

When you're ready, complete today's walk by returning along the same course. You may choose to vary the route and see some of the sights missed on the first pass.

Walk #2: From Fort Point across the Golden Gate Bridge
Walk #3: From Fort Point to Baker Beach

Using Fort Point as a base, *Easy Walkers* have their choice of treks. At the foot of the Bridge you have the option of walking north across the majestic Golden Gate towards Marin County or heading southwest along the rugged San Francisco Headlands, passing a series of late 19th-century batteries on your way to the Presidio's Baker Beach.

Directions: To reach Fort Point, head west on Doyle Drive from Lombard Street or Marina Boulevard on the Golden Gate Bridge approach. Head right at the Golden Gate National Recreation Area exit, before reaching the bridge toll booth. Veer right at the first stop sign and then left at Lincoln. When you reach Long Avenue make another left and follow the signs to Fort Point. Park in the lot at the Fort or near the fishing pier located at the west end of Crissy Field.

Start: Ascend the wooded pathway opposite the restrooms between the fishing pier and Fort Point. On the idyllic first leg, walkers initially climb through a lush area heavily forested with cypress, pine, and eucalyptus trees sprouting from beds of ivy. At the top several footpaths lead to the base of the bridge. Don't worry about getting lost, most lead to the same spot, and you may even stumble upon hidden military relics such as Battery East, the site of five large cannons built in the early 1890s.

These two walks diverge when you reach the pedestrian entrance to the bridge. Restrooms are located near the Roundhouse gift shop and at the turn around points on each walk. Picnic facilities on Walk #3 are located at Baker Beach. Both walks, but especially on the bridge, encounter strong winds. Dress accordingly.

Walk #2: Across the Golden Gate Bridge

Walking Easy Time
1 hour

One of the longest and most beautiful suspension bridges in the world, the Golden Gate Bridge, masterfully engineered by Joseph Strauss, was completed after four and a half years in

1937. Motorists, bicyclists, and pedestrians travel 260 feet above the Bay's surface. Note, before venturing onto the Golden Gate Bridge, that bicyclists are restricted to using one side during the week and the other on weekends. Pedestrians can walk either side, but be prepared to face bicycle traffic on one leg of the journey.

The ultimate viewpoint, the Bridge offers a great look at the Bay, the cities that rim it, Alcatraz, and Angel islands. Sailboats add life to the Bay especially on weekends and clear days when you can also view the distant East Bay hills. On the Marin side, enjoy the headlands park before returning to San Francisco.

On the west side you'll have a commanding view of the city's Pacific gateway. Vessels heading in across Potato Patch Shoalty make their grand entrance. Flanked by historic forts north and south, this beautiful harbor entrance is particularly memorable at sunset.

Going from the eastern to the western side or vice versa is easy; just follow the paths beneath the base of the bridge at either end.

Walk #3: To Baker Beach

Walking Easy Time
1 hour

Follow the bicycle trail leading underneath the Golden Gate towards the Pacific. Before you reach the pedestrian walkway atop the bridge, veer right, following signs for the Coastal Trail. Walking through these serpentine cliffs known as the San Francisco Headlands, you'll see ahead the rocky shores of Lands End. Windswept cypress trees, toyon bushes, ivy, and ice plant dominate the coastal landscape. Remnants of Battery Cranston and Marcus Miller are seen on your left. Part of Fort Winfield Scott, both were constructed in the late 1890s.

The path winds inland, paralleling the Presidio's Lincoln

Boulevard. Along the way you'll pass the eastern facade of Batteries Boutelle, Godfrey, and West, which also harbored guns or cannons prior to the Second World War.

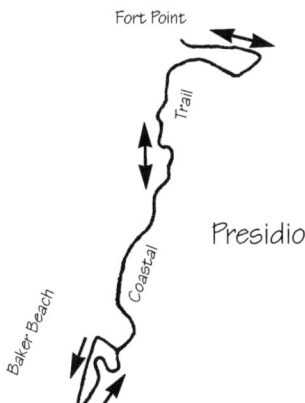

As the trail descends towards Baker Beach, proceed left, away from Battery Crosby. Here you have the option of taking the wooden steps descending steeply toward the beach, or following the Coastal Trail to the Baker Beach parking lot. We recommend taking the initial pathway down (please exercise caution especially in bad weather). Walk along the shore toward the southern end of the beach, picnic in the pleasant cypress grove east of the parking lot, and return via the inland route along the Coastal Trail again.

(An additional note of caution: Many people at Baker Beach bathe nude. If you find this disturbing then avoid the shore entirely and remain on the Coastal Trail.)

Walk #4: Coastal Trail between Sutro Heights and China Beach

Walking Easy Time
2 hours

The Coastal Trail between the Cliff House in Sutro Heights and China Beach is a gentle, level traverse atop those rocky cliffs eerily known as Lands End. In a city with no shortage of memorable vistas, this lovely spot is among the best. Perched above the Pacific, you'll enjoy views of the windswept Pacific, marine mammals, fishing vessels, sailboats, and giant freighters steaming in from the Far East. The scene of numerous shipwrecks, this rocky corner offers spectacular northeastern views of the Golden Gate Bridge and the rugged Marin Headland wilderness. This route is a photographer's dream. Be sure to bring your camera on this one. (Note: There are many spur trails that traverse the side of the cliffs below the Coastal Trail. While they appear interesting to explore, all are unstable and dangerous. Don't try them!)

Directions: From downtown San Francisco, follow Geary Boulevard west, across the city. Just before reaching the Cliff House, perched on the Pacific, park in the lot on the right at Merrie Way and Point Lobos Avenue.

This three-mile walk does not take much time, but it's ideally situated near many popular San Francisco sights such as the Palace of the Legion of Honor, the Cliff House, Sutro Baths and Garden. Plan on spending the better part of your day here. Restrooms are located at the Cliff House and we encourage walkers to picnick in Sutro Heights Garden either at the beginning or end of today's stroll.

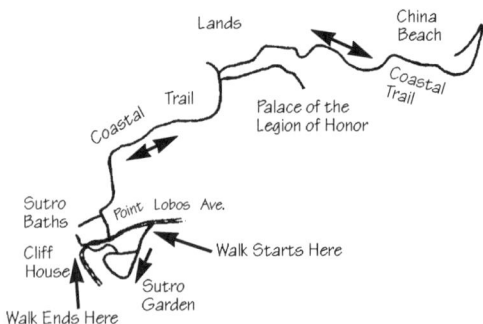

S t a r t : Today's easy walk begins with a brief, yet leisurely jaunt through Sutro Heights Garden located at 48th and Point Lobos avenues. The estate of millionaire and one-time mayor of San Francisco, Adolf Sutro, this garden was far more lavish at the beginning of the century (employing 16 full time gardeners) than it is today. Nonetheless, the grand lawns, flower beds, palm trees, and statuary give the park the kind of grandeur you won't want to miss. From the stone parapet located on the west side of the park you can look down on the Cliff House, Seal Rocks, and Ocean Beach. It's quite a view!

When you've thoroughly explored the park and are ready to proceed, follow the spur trail north of the parapet leading down to a small parking lot. Cross Point Lobos Avenue and descend the paved ramp towards the Sutro Baths ruins.

This extravagant late 19th-century natatorium, encased in glass, could accommodate up to 25,000 people. Several swimming tanks, now rainfall basins, remain separated from the Pacific only by a narrow rock jetty.

After exploring this area, take the stairs that lead east to the parking lot above. Located at the far, northern end of the lot you'll find access to the Coastal Trail where a small, dirt path leads walkers through a cypress grove before reaching the main walkway.

Turn left onto the larger trail and head through San Francisco's Headlands, curving around Lands End before reaching China Beach. Windswept cypress trees and low coastal scrub line the spacious, level walkway. This portion of the trail is where Sutro, transporting downtown guests to his clifftop mansion, built his railroad line. Nearby, a spur path leads up towards Vista Point and the *U.S.S. San Francisco* Memorial where you'll find yet another panoramic view of the Golden Gate Bridge and the Pacific Ocean.

Before reaching a set of ascending wooden steps, you'll notice a driveway veering right and inland. This path is one of several, leading towards the Palace of the Legion of Honor, a great museum in an impressionist setting (see pp. 42-43 for more information). Close to this detour, you'll also notice steps leading down towards Mile Rock Beach where many ships met an untimely end.

Continue to the flight of wooden steps leading up and inland through a thick patch of cypress and shady eucalyptus trees. Head out and down towards the coast where the trail narrows, passing through toyon, mugwort, and dune tansy. At what appears to be the end of the trail (the dirt path ends just beyond this point), *Easy Walkers* approach another wooded viewing platform. You can either turn around here or follow El Camino Del Mar towards China Beach.

View beautiful homes as you pass through a quiet residential district. When El Camino Del Mar breaks right, continue left, descending towards the shore. Turn left again (sharply) at Sea

Cliff Avenue which leads to China Beach. One of the few safe places to swim in San Francisco (if you can stand near freezing temperatures), China Beach is a pleasant, protected cove which is perfect for children and picnics. Named for the Chinese men who fished just offshore, it is suspected they also smuggled Chinese immigrants into the city.

Return along the same scenic route, exploring any of the sites missed on the trip out. After returning to the Sutro Baths area, head down Point Lobos Avenue to the Cliff House. Here you can tour the GGNRA visitor center, learn more about Adolf Sutro, and take a closer look at Seal Rocks (a misnomer as they actually harbor California and Steller Sea Lions). The House today is actually the third built on this site. Now a touristy ocean front restaurant, the first Cliff House, built in the 1860s, was an exclusive resort/gambling casino which acquired a checkered reputation before burning down in the 1890s. Adolf Sutro purchased the property, building an elaborate eight-story mansion, visited by many celebrities and several presidents. It too was leveled by a fire in 1907, after surviving the 1906 earthquake. The GGNRA acquired the property in 1977, and today Sutro's legacy can be enjoyed by anyone who likes to walk by the sea.

Walk #5: Golden Gate Park

Walking Easy Time
2-6 hours

To see it is to believe it: over 1000 acres of countryside cultivated from a vast wasteland of sand. This is Golden Gate Park! No one thought it could be done when the idea was sparked in 1868, not even Frederick Law Olmstead, the famous landscape architect and designer of New York's Central Park. Not only did William Hammond Hall and John McLaren do it, but the final product astonished the cynics. These two men could make anything grow in their giant garden. Hall began the project in 1871 but resigned five years later to free himself of the political bureaucracy. Before leaving, though, he named as his successor, John McLaren, who took over as Superintendent in 1890 and worked tirelessly for the next 53 years. The goal was rusticity rather than refinement and both men fought endlessly against encroaching development.

Buildings and statuary were seen as hideous distractions to the natural haven they wanted to create. Even though McLaren tried his best to hide statues in the brush, there are so many commemorating poets, philosophers, musicians, presidents, revolutionaries, etc., it's hard not to notice them. Still, the natural landscape predominates. The rustic beauty of the sloping hills and cozy meadows, gorgeous groves, streams, and quaint lakes belies the fact that everything you see was manmade.

Here you'll explore an urban botanic community with impressive species from the Bay Area and beyond. In addition to native redwoods and cypress trees, eucalyptus, Monterey pine, and numerous other species from around the world are planted here. Flowers, ranging from camellias, dahlias, fuchsias, magnolia, rhododendrons, roses, and tulips, bloom year round. Activities in the park are countless. From lawn bowling to horse back riding, to flyfish casting, you are never short of choices. With so much to see and offer, it's impossible to do it all in a single day. Twenty-seven miles of trails lead you through this park. But don't limit yourself to a single course. Discover the park for yourself, purposely get lost and explore every nook and cranny.

If this sounds overwhelming, we've started you off with a sample course below—a humble introduction to one of the most spectacular parks in the world. Begin here and then improvise.

Directions: Golden Gate Park is accessed via Highway 101 north. Exit Fell Street west and continue until you reach the park. You'll know you're near when the panhandle appears on your left. Remain in the right hand lanes which enter the park (John F. Kennedy Boulevard) after Fell crosses Stanyan Street.

From downtown San Francisco take either Turk or Geary streets west. Turn left on Stanyan Street, and enter the park by turning right on John F. Kennedy Drive.

Park on John F. Kennedy Drive, shortly after entering the park.

If you're using public transport, take the #38 bus from Union Square to 6th Street and Geary, then transfer onto the #44 bus to the park.

We've laid out a sample route, taking you past several sites that invite exploration. Plan on spending a whole day at the park: visit the museums, wander the gardens, people watch in the Music Concourse, and nap in the meadows. The picnicking possibilities are countless.

Start: After parking, head first to McLaren Lodge where the director lived during his long career as Superintendent. This building now serves as park headquarters. Although it is closed on weekends, you can still pick up a map from a dispenser outside the Lodge. Begin today's walk by taking a closer look at the Conservatory of Flowers. Lovely manicured lawns, flower arrangements that intermittently spell out friendly messages, and regal palm trees grace the exterior of this striking, Victorian-style, glass structure. Built in 1879 and modeled after England's Kew Gardens, this California Historical Landmark encases a tropical paradise of lilies, orchids, ferns, and more.

Continue west on John F. Kennedy Drive, remaining on the right side of the road. Here, after crossing the intersection with Conservatory Drive West, you'll pass a small fledgling titled the George Washington Elm. Giant toyon bushes, bursting with bright, miniature red bulbs in autumn, appear on the right as you pass by.

On the left hand side of the road, crossing Kennedy Drive, visit the John McLaren Memorial Rhododendron Dell. Commemorating the park's papa, this is a peaceful 20-acre enclave where McLaren liked to walk. If you choose to explore further, and are visiting in the Spring, you're likely to find a colorful riot of 70- to 80-year-old Himalayan rhododendrons. Just beyond the Dell, still on Kennedy Drive, look for one of many slightly hidden statues. Find the Scottish poet, Robert Burns, standing tall. Lines inscribed at the base of the statue are taken from "To a Mountain Daisy".

Turning left at the next intersection, Hagiwara Tea Garden Drive leads *Easy Walkers* to the Music Concourse, site of the 1894 California Midwinter Fair. All around the Concourse you'll see statues of stately figures such as Ulysses S. Grant, Junipero Serra, Thomas Starr King, Cervantes, Beethoven, and the Irish patriot, Robert Emmet. Sycamore trees and tai-chi enthusiasts stud the center. Concerts are offered at Spreckels Music Temple—located at the southwestern end of the Concourse.

This site is also flanked by some of San Francisco's best museums. Circle counter clockwise to reach the complex that is joint home to the M. H. de Young and Asian Art museums. Gracing the facade is Earl Cummings's sculpture of a young boy and mountain lion titled *Pool of Enchantment*.

Across the Concourse is the California Academy of Sciences, home of the Morrison Planetarium, Steinhart Aquarium, and the Natural History Museum. (See pp. 43-44 for more details on the museums in Golden Gate Park.)

Exit the Concourse via the right hand side of the stage, passing the famed Japanese Tea Gardens. Planted in 1894 for the Midwinter Exposition's Japanese Village, this peaceful enclave, set amid splendid cherry trees (blooming in April), bonsai gardens, delicate footbridges, and ponds sheltering gold and black carp, showcases a Shinto pagoda, "peace" lantern, and teahouse.

Turn right at the intersection (Martin Luther King Drive) to reach Strybing Arboretum and Botanical Gardens. Don't shortchange, for these magnificent 70 acres feature plants from around the world. Too many visitors make the mistake of overlooking this gem.

Allow plenty of time to enjoy unique spots like the fragrance garden filled with medicinal and culinary herbs labeled in braille, and the California native garden. There's a grove of California redwood trees and you can even see the Dawn Redwood, a rare Chinese species—it's the only one found outside of California and southern Oregon.

A quarter of a mile further on, after passing patches of baby blue eyes, follow signs right, towards doughnut-shaped Stow

Lake and proceed clockwise around its outer shores. A boathouse is situated on the lake's opposite shore where you can rent paddle and row boats. There is also a snack bar.

Cross the stone bridge and continue clockwise, this time along the inner shore. When the pathway begins ascending take the right hand road to the summit of Strawberry Hill. The highest point in the park at 428 feet, the hill was named for the wild strawberries that once grew on its slopes. It doesn't take long to get to the top where views extend out to the Farallon Islands, Mount Tamalpais, and on especially clear days, Mount Diablo. At the summit, a small reservoir feeds Huntington Falls. For a closer look at this cascade, head toward the small wooden bridge descending the steps on your right.

To leave Strawberry Hill head across the wooden bridge and follow the cement steps. The stairway brings you to the base of the hill and a cement bridge.

After crossing the bridge, turn right, following the outer shore. Before completely circling the Lake, take the small spur path on the left (200 yards past the bridge). This pleasant short cut leads through a shady grove of cypress and redwoods back to the intersection of Martin Luther King Drive and Hagiwara Tea Garden Drive. Cross Hagiwara, and continue on Martin Luther King Drive towards 9th Avenue.

On your left, nestled snugly behind the California Academy of Science, find the Shakespeare Garden. Buffs of the famous bard will spot flowers mentioned in his works.

Turn left on Middle Drive which provides a pleasant return to John F. Kennedy Drive. On the right you'll notice the Aids Memorial Grove currently under cultivation. Turn right past the tennis courts to reach your car.

Walk #6: Fort Funston - Sunset Trail

Walking Easy Time
30 minutes

Windswept sand dunes and rugged, serpentine cliffs, reach heights of 200 feet at Fort Funston, reflecting an image of San Francisco's landscape before it became a late 19th-century metropolis. Located at the southern end of Ocean Beach, this area became a strategic defense site at the turn of the century and remained so well into the Cold War.

Visitors can continue to explore the remains of Battery Davis, constructed prior to World War II. But other military installations, such as the NIKE missile battery, now buried under the parking lot, are hidden from view.

Steady winds and towering bluffs provide an ideal locale for human flight. Watch daring hangliders soar over the Pacific from the wooden viewing deck at the west end of the parking lot. You can also create your own low altitude adventure by following one of the Fort's many handsome spur trails. *Easy Walkers* will enjoy exploring up close every nook and cranny of this unique landscape. And for children, an environmental education center is set up at the southern end of the Fort.

Directions: The easiest way to get to Fort Funston is to travel south on Great Highway paralleling Ocean Beach. Turn right on Skyline Boulevard (State Highway 35), and travel an additional mile to the Fort's entrance. Park in the large lot to your right.

The length of today's trek really depends on you. Sunset Trail, marking the southernmost section of the GGNRA's Coastal Trail, is a short, paved route with several branches. For longer treks, walkers can exit Fort Funston and continue northbound along that expansive stretch called Ocean Beach, or remain within the fort, exploring a maze of spur trails ascending clifftops and leading down toward the shore.

This is also a dog walkers haunt. If you are the least bit uncomfortable around roaming dogs this probably isn't the place for you.

Restrooms are located near the parking lot, but picnic facilities are scarce at Fort Funston.

Start: To the right of the Wooden viewing deck, *Easy Walkers* will find Sunset Trail, a mile-long paved path ringing Battery Davis. Built in 1938, this was the first casemated battery, after which many others were modeled, harboring two mammoth, sixteen-inch, 146-ton guns. To guard against an aerial attack the Battery was concealed under a coastal wilderness of ice-plant, toyon, and wind-sculptured cypress trees remaining today. In addition to orange poppies and yellow lupine, sand yerbene, seaside daisies, and mock heather are some of the unique spring wildflowers you will also see at Fort Funston. We suggest taking the eastern route around the Battery which promises pleasant, elevated views of Lake Merced. You'll also be able to rest at convenient benches scattered along the trail. Upon reaching the north end of the Battery, spur trails branch east to Skyline Boulevard, west toward the shore, and north toward Ocean Beach. Here you can wander, exploring Fort Funston's magnificent landscape, to your heart's content.

NORTH BAY

Few cities are more walkable than San Francisco. And when it's time to get out of town, you'll also enjoy exploring the mountains, valleys, and coastal retreats found north of town in Marin, Sonoma, and Napa Counties.

From the Marin Headlands overlooking the Golden Gate, to the many splendors of Jack London's Valley of the Moon retreat, this is a region that offers the very best of California. We go there all the time to enjoy the coast, the wine country, the baylands and, best of all, the splendid isolation available just an hour from the heart of the city.

Like Redwoods? Got 'em. Want to stroll from winery to winery? No problem. Looking for a mountain that offers panoramic views of the entire region? Of course. Island lovers, wildflower junkies, bird watchers, in fact just about anyone serious about the great outdoors will find themselves at home in this fascinating region.

Enough glittering generalities. Let's get oriented to help you begin enjoying all our favorites and perhaps discover a few of your own.

A good place to begin is Point Reyes National Seashore where Sir Frances Drake landed the *Golden Hind* in 1579. Or perhaps you'd rather begin in Sonoma where the Pomo and coastal Miwok tribes flourished until the missionaries arrived in the early 19th century. A rebellion that led to the torching of the mission prompted the Mexican government to send new leadership. The region's new commander in chief was General Mariano Guadalupe Vallejo, an important figure in California history.

While the Mexicans dominated this period in regional history, another world power also made a play for control of the area's lucrative fishery. In 1812 a crew of Russians and native Alaskans set up a base at Sonoma County's Fort Ross. The Czar even issued a ukase, closing the Pacific Coast north of San Francisco to all non-Russian ships. Ultimately Washington, via the Monroe Doctrine, forced Moscow to sell out its interest in the region.

This left the territory firmly in control of Mexico's General Vallejo who, ironically, began campaigning for California's annexation by the United States. After Mexico City granted California to Washington in 1848, Vallejo enlisted in the region's nascent wine making industry.

Today most visitors are attracted to the wine making region of Napa and Sonoma County by the opportunity to sample fine wines for little or nothing. But you'd be making a mistake if you didn't take time out to visit some of the region's parks and historic sites which are prime destinations for *Easy Walkers*.

Among them are little known finds like Bartholomew Memorial Park where you'll find a re-creation of Agoston Haraszthy's mid 19th-century villa. This Hungarian immigrant brought the region's first vineyard cuttings from Europe. He also helped persuade many of his old-world vintner friends to join him in the fertile fields of the Napa and Sonoma valleys.

A region also rich in literary history, the North Bay nurtured the talents of visitors like Robert Louis Stevenson who arrived broke and ill with tuberculosis in 1880. He convalesced north of Napa on Mount Saint Helena with his wife in the abandoned bunkhouse of the Silverado Mine. The story of those days is told in his book, *The Silverado Squatters.*

Another writer who lived and died in this region was Jack London. His Sonoma County lands are the centerpiece of one of this section's finest walks.

In a region famous for its seismic activity, there are many intriguing ways to see nature's handiwork closeup. One of the easiest is Point Reyes' earthquake nature trail. During the 1906 earthquake land here shifted northward as much as 21 feet. You can see excellent visual evidence of this astonishing offset on the self-guiding trail.

Marin County, one of the region's most fashionable suburban enclaves, was originally the domain of the Coast Miwok who lived nomadically. They dominated the area until the early 19th century when whalers took control of their waters. Decimated by white man's diseases such as smallpox, the Native

Americans across the North Bay lost their territory to the missionaries and Mexican settlers.

During the Gold Rush era a new generation of settlers tapped into the region's redwood resources to provide the board feet necessary to build a good share of San Francisco. Later the redwoods sparked the county's nascent tourist business. San Franciscans came over by ferry to enjoy excursion rail rides through the remaining redwood groves. One of the most popular routes was known as The Crookedest Railroad in the World.

The opening of the Golden Gate bridge in 1937 eased access to the North Bay and helped popularize its many attractions. Muir Woods, named for Sierra Club founder John Muir, became the region's leading attraction and, in 1945, site of the conference that led to the creation of the United Nations.

Marin is also the home of Mount Tamalpais State Park where visitors can enjoy walk-in camps and a hillside amphitheater where plays and musicals are staged in May and June. Expansion of the park in the 1950s, thanks to the efforts of conservationists like Ansel Adams, protected much of this region from development. Among the many delights of Mount Tamalpais are five small lakes.

Perhaps the region's most important resource and the world's largest urban park is the 114-square-mile Golden Gate National Recreation Area. Extending from San Francisco north to Point Reyes, this land embraces an extensive trail network, handsome forests, seashore campgrounds, and beautiful overlooks.

A great place to spot a black-tailed deer or a fox, this region is a backyard wilderness that protects the North Bay against wholesale development of its finest landscape. It's a monument to the foresight of local congressmen like Phillip Burton and William Mailliard who led the successful campaign to create this preserve in 1972.

The largest national recreation area unit is the Point Reyes National Seashore, the first national park property to be repurchased from private land owners. Other units located in West Marin and well worth a visit include Stinson Beach, Tennessee Valley, and the east slope of Olema Valley.

Although Marin is famous for its affluent suburbs satirized in books and movies such as *The Serial*, about 40 percent of the region remains rural and agricultural. As in neighboring Napa and Sonoma Counties, tight zoning and extensive parklands have protected the region's scenic assets which are the focus of our easy walks.

Probably the best known community in the North Bay is Napa, hub of the region's winemaking industry. A perfect place to hike, bike, go horseback riding or ballooning, this river town has served tourists for more than a century. With roots in leather tanning, stone masonry, cattle ranching, farming, and viticulture, Napa was first reached by pioneer steamer. While wine is the principal attraction today, early visitors came to sample the valley's healing mineral waters. The valley's first spa, White Sulfur Springs, opened in 1852. North of Napa, the community of Calistoga was turned into a spa town that flourishes to this day.

Some of region's best walks are found at landmarks like Bale Grist Mill State Park where visitors can see an 1846 waterwheel mill used to grind corn. State park units are also popular in the neighboring Sonoma Valley. Like Napa, the Sonoma region is rich in history. The historic mission area and the state's oldest winery, Buena Vista, offer visitors a chance to enjoy this community's unreconstructed past. Sonoma, incidentally, is the Native American word for Valley of the Moon.

To the north, the Russian River region is another popular resort area that has served tourists for over a century. This forested resort community has everything from the exclusive Bohemian Grove (where famous businessmen and politicians retreat each summer) to public beaches jammed on weekends. More spacious than Muir Woods, Armstrong Redwoods State Reserve is a major preserve north of Guerneville.

The Feel of Walks in the North Bay

Without many urban distractions, *Easy Walkers* will quickly feel at home in the semi wilderness of the North Bay. Here, you'll experience a wide range of natural terrain from the coastal landscape of Point Reyes National Seashore to the redwoods of Muir Woods and Armstrong State Reserve. Explore the heights of Marin County's Mount Tamalpais, the lofty peaks bridging Sonoma and Napa counties, and the gorgeous depths of valley basins.

Transportation to the North Bay

From San Francisco take Highway 101 over the Golden Gate Bridge. To reach coastal Marin County take the exit for State Highway 1. Other Marin communities such as Sausalito, Mill Valley, and San Rafael exit off 101. To reach Sonoma, continue north on 101, take State Highway 37 east to State Highway 121 north, and finally State Highway 12 north which passes through Sonoma. To reach Napa take 121 to State Highway 29 north.

From the East Bay, take Interstate 80 north to 37 west. Then head north on 29 all the way to Napa. Follow this route to Sonoma as well, but exit northwest on State Highway 12 before reaching the city of Napa.

For those interested in public transit, Golden Gate Transit (Fremont Street, between Market and Mission streets; (415) 453-2100 or 332-6600) offers service from San Francisco to Stinson Beach, Olema, Point Reyes Visitor Center and Inverness, Sonoma, and Santa Rosa.

Greyhound also offers bus service to both Napa and Sonoma.

Activities and Excursions in the North Bay

1. Headlands Center for the Arts. (Open from noon to 5 daily; (415) 331-2887.) Here artists are invited each year to set up studios, create, and occasionally exhibit at public gatherings.

Directions: Located at Fort Barry, off Bunker Road in the Marin Headlands.

2. Green Gulch Farm and Zen Center. (415) 383-3134. A Zen retreat for those seeking spiritual illumination through eastern religions. Guests are invited to stay overnight or visit for the day, joining in tea ceremonies, lectures, meditations, and gardening.

Directions: located at 1601 Shoreline Highway (State Highway 1).

3. Bay Area Discovery Museum. (Open 10 to 5 Wednesday through Sunday in the winter; 10 to 5 Tuesday through

Sunday in the summer; (415) 487-4398.) Created exclusively for children and families, five buildings with a media center and science lab host hands-on and changing exhibits. Indoor art workshops and outdoor activities are carefully planned to stimulate children's creativity and artistic awareness.

Directions: Located at 557 East Fort Baker in Sausalito.

4. Sonoma Plaza. *Mission Francisco Solano* (1st and Spain streets at the northeast corner of the Plaza; (707) 938-1519.) The last and northernmost mission built in California, Sonoma Mission is a State Historic Monument. Today it doubles as a museum, exhibiting 19th-century watercolors by Chris Jorgenson.

Lachryma Montis is the former home of General Mariano Vallejo who laid out the town of Sonoma in 1834. Many of the adobes dotting the square date back to Mexican rule.

The Swiss Hotel, Toscano Hotel, Vasquez House, old Mexican barracks, Bear Flag Monument, Depot Museum, and Nash-Patton Adobe are all worth a visit.

Directions: Located in downtown Sonoma off State Highway 29, and bounded by Napa and Spain streets, 1st Street east and 1st Street west.

> ☞ **HINT: Delicatessens, gourmet, and specialty shops, ideal for creating the perfect picnic, surround the square.**

> ☞ **HINT: Antique lovers will feel right at home in Sonoma County which is dotted with quaint, quality shops.**

5. Viansa Winery and Italian Marketplace. (707) 935-4700. The first major winery on your way into Sonoma from San Francisco, this Tuscan-style establishment offers excellent tasting, dining, and special musical events. A beautiful, if windswept, setting.

Directions: 25200 Arnold Drive (State Highway 121), south of Sonoma.

6. Buena Vista. (707) 938-1266. California's oldest (circa 1857) premium winery is a short drive east of the Plaza. Blessed with a beautiful cellar, the winery has lovely picnic grounds and features a Shakespeare festival on Sundays during the summer months.

Directions: Located at 18000 Old Winery Road not far from downtown Sonoma.

7. Gundlach-Bundschu. (707) 938-5277. Another popular tasting room. While there are no tours, you can watch the crush taking place from the tasting area. Special events include weekend Shakespeare plays in the summer months.

Directions: 2000 Denmark Street, near downtown Sonoma.

8. Ravenswood. (707) 938-1960. Located in the Sonoma Hills, this small, intimate winery with a stone facade specializes in Zinfandels and Merlots. Tours are available by appointment only. Enjoy the vineyard picnic area.

Directions: 18701 Gehricke Road north of the town plaza.

9. Cline Cellars. (707) 935-4310. Set in a mid-1800s farmhouse, visitors also sample mustards and chocolate while sipping wine. Scenic ponds dot the grounds making for a pleasant place to picnic.

Directions: 24737 Arnold Drive (State Highway 121).

10. Valley of the Moon Winery. 707 996-6941. One of Sonoma's older wineries, the vineyards date back to the 1850s. Sample excellent wines in a wood-frame building overlooking Sonoma Creek and surrounded by fragrant bay laurel trees.

Directions: 777 Madrone Road in Glen Ellen, north of Sonoma.

11. Chateau St. Jean. (707) 833-4134. Premium wines are served in a contemporary winery building. An excellent self-guided tour. Less crowded but fully the equal of Napa Valley's better known wineries.

Directions: 8555 Sonoma Highway (12), just past Kenwood.

12. Hot air ballooning is one of the best ways to begin your day in the wine country. These scenic trips are an easy way to get an overview of the region you'll be exploring by foot.

Napa Valley Balloons (800) 253-2224 offers daily departures from the Domaine Chandon Winery. The narrated dawn rides take about an hour. Your exact route depends on the winds. Champagne brunch is served after your flight.

For the names of other balloon flight operators call the **Professional Balloon Pilots Association** (707) 944-8793.

> ☞ **HINT: Napa's Silverado Trail is a scenic alternative to State Highway 29. Located a mile east and running parallel to 29, this route takes you to off the beaten path wineries.**

13. Napa Valley Wine Train. (707) 253-2111. For $55 you can enjoy a three-hour, 36-mile, turn-of-the-century Pullman car excursion through the Valley. Sample different wines while enjoying a champagne brunch, gourmet lunch, or four-course dinner. Reservations required.

Directions: 1275 McKinstry Street in Napa.

14. Hess Collection Winery. (707) 255-1144. An excellent place for art lovers to sample wine, the Hess collection hosts an impressive gallery adjacent to the tasting room. The contemporary gallery features artists Robert Motherwell, Frank Stella, and Francis Bacon. The winery is best known for its Cabernets grown on the Mt. Veeder estate.

Directions: 4411 Redwood Road in the western hills of the southern end of Napa Valley.

15. S. Anderson Vineyard. (800) 428-2259. This 120-acre vineyard featuring Chardonnays and Pinot Noirs is best known for its Champagne Caves. More than 400,000 bottles are aged here. Anderson's champagnes are frequently served at White House events. This Georgian Colonial winery is well worth a tour.

Directions: 1473 Yountville Crossroad in Yountville.

16. Stag's Leap Wine Cellars. (707) 944-2020. Not to be confused with another Napa Valley winery, Stags' Leap Winery, this Stag's Leap is perched on the hillside just off the Silverado Trail in an idyllic oak grove. Featuring several varieties of red and white wines, the winery offers tasting daily.

Directions: 5766 Silverado Trail near Yountville.

17. Merryvale. (707) 963-2225. Built on the site of Napa Valley's first post prohibition winery, Merryvale's handsome tasting cellars are a great place to try Chardonnays, Cabernets, Merlots, and a dessert wine called Antigua. Don't miss the handsome cask room with its century-old, 2,000-gallon casks.

Directions: 1000 Main Street in St. Helena.

18. Chateau Montelena. (707) 942-5105. Located north of town on the way to Robert Louis Stevenson State Park, this winery gives you a chance to taste fine Chardonnays and Cabernets in a charming castle. It's located next to a small lake with pavilions done in an Asian motif.

Directions: 1429 Tubbs Lane in Calistoga.

☞ **HINT: For maps and additional information about Sonoma and Napa Valley wineries, look in shops, wineries, and the respective visitor centers or chambers of commerce.**

19. Calistoga. If you'd like to get down and dirty why not drive on up to the century-old resort town of Calistoga and hop in one of the mud baths. Or, if you prefer, consider one of the hot spring spas located in this community known for its geysers and petrified forest. Napa Valley's northernmost community, Calistoga is the kind of place where you can soak for hours, enjoy a glider ride, visit a nearby memorial to Robert Louis Stevenson, and take your pick of fine restaurants.

Among your choices are **Calistoga Spa** at 1006 Washington Street (707) 942-6269, and **Dr. Wilkinson's Hot Springs** at 1507 Lincoln Avenue (707) 942-4102. Created by millionaire Sam Brannan, Calistoga is also the home of the **Sharpsteen Museum** where you can learn more about the region and the career of Robert Louis Stevenson. It's located at

1311 Washington Street (707) 942-5911. Be sure to visit the intriguing **Petrified Forest** at 4100 Petrified Forest Road, six miles northwest of town (707) 942-6667.

Accommodations

The Continental Alta Mira Hotel - 125 Bulkley Avenue, Sausalito; (415) 332-1350 [$70-170]. This Spanish-style villa first opened in 1927 and continues to please visitors today. Experience city comfort in the Sausalito Hills just minutes from the Marin Headland wilderness. Comfortable rooms and a terrace restaurant, graced with elevated views of the San Francisco skyline, make the Alta Mira a romantic retreat. [Proprietor: Mrs. William Wachter]

Mountain Home Inn - 810 Panoramic Highway in Mill Valley; (415) 381-9000, fax (415) 381-3615 [$131-215]. Ten rustic rooms, each with modern amenities and private terrace grace this upscale inn ideally nestled in the heart of Marin's wilderness. Literally minutes away from Muir Woods, Mount Tam, the Headlands, and Point Reyes, this fashionable retreat also boasts an intimate restaurant with outdoor dining on the deck.

Casa del Mar Bed & Breakfast - 37 Belvedere Avenue, Stinson Beach; (415) 868-2124 [$100-225]. An extraordinary garden first cultivated in the 1930s and still blossoming with passion flowers, roses, cacti, palm, and fruit trees, borders the walkway leading up to this coastal bed and breakfast. Enjoy innovative breakfasts prepared by innkeeper Rick Klein while relaxing in this Mediterranean-style villa, close to Point Reyes National Seashore, Mount Tamalpais, Muir Woods, and the Marin Headlands.

Roundstone Farm - 9940 Sir Francisco Drake Boulevard, just outside the town of Olema; (415) 663-1020 [$115-125]. Situated on a ten-acre Arabian and Connemara horse ranch, this farm is the place to see deer, red-winged blackbirds, and other country critters. Rooms with private baths and fireplaces are tastefully decorated and especially cozy. A full country-gourmet breakfast is served each morning on the deck or in the intimate dining room featuring splendid views of the valley wilderness. [Innkeeper: Inger Fisher]

Ten Inverness Way - P.O. Box 63, Inverness; (415) 669-1648 [$110-160]. Bring a book if you decide to stay at Ten Inverness Way. After a long day of walking at Point Reyes, you can return and catch up on your reading while curled up next to the cozy fireplace or reclining outside in the garden. Guests are invited to soak privately in the garden hottub and feast on an exceptional breakfast. [Proprietor: Mary Davies]

Sonoma Chalet - 18935 Fifth Street West, near downtown Sonoma; (707) 938-3129 [$75-135]. Less than a mile away from the town square, Sonoma Chalet, built in the 1940s, is a Swiss-style farmhouse set on a three-acre wilderness. Three comfy, country-style rooms are located in the farmhouse with three additional private cottages dotting the grounds. Featured in "Best Places to Kiss in the Bay Area," this romantic hideaway is the perfect base for Sonoma County walks. [Proprietor: Joe Leese]

Gaige House Inn - 13540 Arnold Drive in Glen Ellen; (707) 935-0237, fax (707) 935-6411 [$100-225]. This Italianate Queen Anne built in the late 1800s by Albert Gaige is decorated with abstract art and unusual antiques (a Balinese armoire). Eight comfortable rooms are available to guests along with a hearty country breakfast. In the late spring and summer months, spend time outdoors in the garden lounging in the hammock. [Innkeeper: Ardath Rouas]

Pygmalion House - 331 Orange Street, Santa Rosa; (707) 526-3407 [$60-70]. Centrally located, this 1880s Victorian is an ideal base for upper Sonoma and Napa county walks. Fully restored and renovated, its name, like Shaw's play, reflects the transformation of this rundown property to landmark status. A country kitchen and private baths with antique claw foot tubs are some of the special features at this delightful B & B. [Innkeeper: Lola L. Wright]

Oliver House Bed and Breakfast Country Inn - 2970 Silverado Trail North, in St. Helena; (707) 963-4089 [$75-195]. Just outside of town, Oliver House is snugly situated in the foothills of St. Helena and offers splendid views of neighboring vineyards. Within walking distance of many wineries and close to Bothe-Napa Valley State Park, this is a convenient retreat, featuring four guest rooms cozily decorated with French and English antiques. [Innkeepers: Richard and Clara Oliver]

La Belle Epoque Bed and Breakfast Inn - 1386 Calistoga Avenue, centrally located in Calistoga's Historic District, Napa Valley; (707) 257-2161 [$110-150]. This Queen Anne Victorian, built in 1893, features a high-tipped roof, gables, and original stained-glass windows. Guests are pampered with a full gourmet breakfast each morning, and wine and hors d'oeuvres served afternoons in the Wine Tasting Room. A decanter of sherry is part of each guestroom's furnishings along with a tasteful collection of period antiques. [Innkeepers: Merlin and Claudia Wedepohl]

Restaurants

Guaymas Restaurant - 5 Main Street in Tiburon, Marin County; (415) 435-6300. An upscale Mexican restaurant in a white stucco, adobe-like setting, Guaymas features cactus tomales and fresh corn tortillas in addition to regional entrees. An outdoor deck, pleasant on summer afternoons, offers splendid views of Angel Island and San Francisco. Reservations recommended.

Lark Creek Inn - 234 Magnolia in Larkspur, Marin County; (415) 924-7766. Located in a rustic setting surrounded by redwoods, this moderately priced restaurant is warm and cozy with dark wood paneling and a brick fireplace. Billed as an American restaurant the wine list contains mostly domestic wines. The food and service here are excellent. The sandwiches offered at lunch are notable. The patio is one of Marin's finest dining spots. Reservations recommended.

Cafe Citti - 9049 Sonoma Highway in Kenwood, Sonoma County; (707) 833-2690. This moderately-priced establishment is popular with locals. Great for carryout, try the rotisserie chicken, pasta selections, and heavenly sweets.

The French Laundry - 6640 Washington Street in Yountville, Napa County; (707) 944-2380. An elegant, upscale restaurant in a beautiful, ivy covered stone building, The French Laundry offers diners a choice of four or five course (each course diligently and innovatively prepared) prix fixe menus. Featured entrees include roasted breast of veal coated with mustard and bread crumbs and topped with polenta and marscapone cheese. A vegetarian option is also offered. Expensive. Reservations required.

Paris Parkside Cafe - 1420 Main Street in St. Helena, Napa County; (707) 963-7566. This downtown St. Helena restaurant is hard to miss and hard to beat. The eclectic menu includes dishes like the grilled basil burger, pesto prawn pizza, and a vegetarian picnic sandwich. For dinner, consider the roasted monkfish wrapped with applewood bacon on chile corn or garlic roasted mussels. Reservations recommended.

Terra - 1345 Railroad Avenue in St. Helena, Napa County; (707) 963-8931. Deluxe and worth it, Terra features dishes like Oakville squab with eggplant goat cheese lasagna, broiled sake marinated sea bass with shrimp dumplings in shiso broth, and lamb and artichoke daube with polenta and tapenade crouton. A beautiful dining room in a historic St. Helena location. Reservations recommended.

Bistro Don Giovanni - 4110 St. Helena Highway (29), in Napa County; (707) 224-3300. Come early to avoid the lines at this trendy and extremely popular Tuscan-style dining room. An overwhelming starter, the fritto misto is a generous portion of crispy rock shrimp, sweet onions, and beans with spicy aioli. Choose from entrees like grilled Sonoma duck breast and seared filet of salmon with buttermilk-mashed potatoes. Lighter fare like beet and spinach salad is also on the menu. Reservations recommended.

North Bay Walks

Walk #1: Marin Headlands - Kirby Cove Trail

Walking Easy Time
1 hour

Miles of uninhabited, rugged, and spectacular shoreline comprise the North Bay's treasured Marin Headlands. Once a strategic coastal defense area, the Marin Headlands fortunately never saw battle, and were relatively untouched. They are now preserved as part of the Golden Gate National Recreation Area. Blessed with natural plant and wildlife activity year round, this is the perfect place for wilderness lovers to observe and explore.

This delightful little walk can easily lead to a half or all-day excursion. After slowly winding your way down into the cove, you won't want to leave this wilderness—adjacent to the Golden Gate.

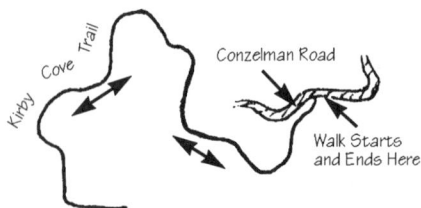

An ideal spot for picnicking, reclining in the shade or sun, or spending time with a good book in a private nook, Kirby Cove is a tranquil North Bay haven that's hard to beat. The only difficulty you'll encounter is finding the trailhead.

Directions: On Highway 101 north, take the first exit off the Golden Gate Bridge, and head west on Conzelman Road. There are several fine outlook points along this single lane road. The trailhead for Kirby Cove is located at the second turnout, immediately beyond Battery Spenser. (If you have some time after today's easy walk, stop at Battery Spenser on your way back for awe-filled close-ups of the Golden Gate that shouldn't be missed.)

Start: Spacious and straight forward, the fire road descends gradually. Near the beginning of the walk, look for remnants of military fortifications below the trail. Spur trails sneak down the chaparral laden hillside for those who want a closer look. Lupine and bright orange poppies soften the rugged coastal seascape. At the cove, you'll be surprised to find a woodsy enclave of redwoods, firs, and ferns so close to the sea. This hideaway is a great place to read, relax, or meditate.

Cove bathrooms are located near the four campsites, and picnic tables strategically dot the area. Once you've had a chance to lunch and leisurely explore the forest and shoreline, return along the same path.

Walk #2: Muir Woods - Muir Woods Nature Trail to Ben Johnson Trail to Dipsea Trail

Walking Easy Time
2½ hours

Nestled snugly between rugged headland cliffs and the slopes of Mount Tamalpais is the popular Muir Woods, where cool redwoods ascend to heavenly heights and *Easy Walkers* explore miles of verdant splendor. What you see at Muir Woods today realizes much of William Kent's turn-of-the-century vision. He and his wife first purchased the land with the dream of building a lodge and drawing tourists. They soon realized, however, that this treasure would be plundered without official protection. In

1908 Kent donated his land, through the Antiquities Act, to the United States Government. This territory was then proclaimed a national monument and named after the famed conservationist, John Muir.

If you can, avoid visiting Muir Woods on the weekends when bus loads of visitors flock to view the spectacular redwoods that grace this beautiful region.

Directions: Drive north on State Highway 1 after exiting Highway 101 in Marin County. After several winding miles the road forks and you'll veer right onto Panoramic Highway, heading towards Mount Tamalpais. Turn left at the first intersection (Muir Woods Road) and descend into the park.

Today's walk explores several diverse life zones. Redwood forests, handsome meadows, and panoramic views are all part of the fun.

Restrooms are found near the visitor center only and picnic facilities are surprisingly scarce. Plan on improvising; Dipsea Trail, flanked by grassy slopes and hosting incomparable views of the Pacific, offers many opportunities for an old-fashioned, picnic-blanket lunch.

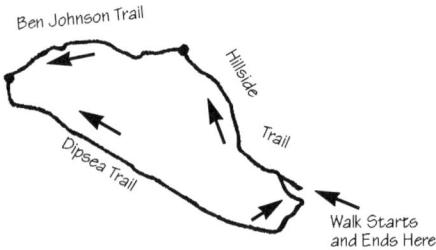

S t a r t :
Begin by exploring the visitor center then cross the first bridge so that Redwood Creek is on your right. The riparian environment is lush with big leaf maple and red alders along the bank of this stream which nurtures coho salmon and steelhead trout. Come springtime, redwood violets and trillium ornament the landscape.

Ben Johnson Trail

Hillside

Trail

Dipsea Trail

Walk Starts
and Ends Here

This section of the Muir Woods Nature Trail, en route to Ben Johnson Trail, is heavily trafficked; but the crowds don't diminish the awesome beauty of virgin coast redwoods rising hundreds of feet above a thick carpet of sword, braken, and licorice fern.

Along the way you'll see California bay laurels lying horizontal with branches stretching longingly towards the sun. From April through September, you won't want to miss the pink redwood sorrel blossoms.

After passing through Bohemian Grove, make a left at the first junction, ascend the wooden steps, and continue to follow signs for Ben Johnson Trail. On the trail, the narrow path leads *Easy Walkers* diagonally up the northeastern slope of the mountain.

You'll pass over makeshift wooden footbridges and through stands of Douglas firs, tanbark oak, and California buckeye trees accenting the stately redwoods. On this trail follow signs toward Dipsea Trail and Stinson Beach.

Near the top, the trail turns into a steep, switchback ascent, intersecting Deer Park Fire Road at the summit. Proceed straight ahead, crossing Deer Park, onto the Dipsea Trail. Twenty yards further on, the Dipsea Trail veers left in the opposite direction of Stinson Beach.

This narrow path initially leads through a mixed evergreen forest where, after another 50 yards, you'll see the twisted and tortured roots of a massive redwood toppled by the wind. The redwood's worst enemy, wind can easily dominate this tree's surprisingly shallow and weak root system.

Dipsea Trail traverses the western slope of the mountain. After exiting the evergreen forest on your left, continue through grassy clearings and chaparral patches, enjoying great views of the Pacific on your right. Dipsea Trail and Deer Park Fire Road cross paths several times over the next mile. Don't worry about getting lost, they lead in the same direction.

Before reaching Muir Woods Road, Dipsea Trail veers left onto a narrow path, entering a lush, fern-lined grove. After feeling like you've just spent several minutes in the heart of the rain forest, exit the grove and cross Redwood Creek. Turn left on the paved trail skimming the outside of the parking lot. This spur trail, paralleling the creek, leads *Easy Walkers* back to the visitor center.

Walk #3: Mount Tamalpais - Pantoll to Matt Davis Trail to Coastal Trail to Willow Camp Fire Road to Laurel Dell Fire Road to Cataract Trail to Old Mine Trail and back to Pantoll

Walking Easy Time
4 hours

Built of sandstone, limestone, schist, chert, and serpentine, 2,571-foot-high Mount Tamalpais (or Mount Tam) is Marin's aerie, a scenic overlook with ocean, bay, and San Francisco views. The mountain is named after the Tamals, the Miwok tribe once based here. The mountain's proximity to the sea, steep slopes, and geologic diversity have created a variety of intriguing life zones. While the headlands were preserved for strategic military reasons, Mount Tam was considered too rugged for development. If you have an affinity for the mountains and the sea, Mount Tamalpais, a woodsy North Bay haven, is the place to be.

Directions: Head west on State Highway 1, off Highway 101 north of the Golden Gate Bridge, and follow signs toward Mount Tamalpais, Muir Woods, and Stinson Beach. After winding for several miles, make a right at the fork onto Panoramic Highway. Remain on this road until you reach the Pantoll Ranger Station and Park Headquarters. Park in any nook along Panoramic or in the lot for a small fee.

This easy walk is comprised of inter-connecting ridge and forest trails forming a scenic, six-mile loop. Although the walk is lengthy, there is little change in elevation. Take advantage of the Laurel Dell picnic area midway into today's hike or find a private picnic spot that suits you.

Start: Find the Matt Davis Trail head by ascending the steps across Panoramic Highway opposite Pantoll Ranger Station. Following the trail marker you'll descend into a shady evergreen grove, crossing several streams along the way. The path leads to a clearing with rewarding views of the Pacific coastline. Beyond this clearing the path approaches a trail intersection—simply continue straight ahead. The Matt Davis Trail heads through shady oak groves and sunny clearings to a fork where you'll veer right.

This new path begins the Coastal Trail and continues along Mount Tam's ridge, cutting through grassy slopes dotted with orange poppies and purple lupine in springtime. With little shade, this is the warmest part of the trek but the ocean breeze is always refreshing.

A mile further on, Coastal Trail intersects Willow Camp Fire Road. Turn right at this intersection and remain on the main road. Ascend 100 yards and veer left onto the narrow trail paralleling the fire road. This route crosses Ridgecrest Boulevard and descends inland, cooling off as the evergreen forest thickens. Willow Camp turns into Laurel Dell Fire Road and leads into a small, sunny clearing. The Laurel Dell picnic area (50 yards straight ahead and on your left) is a convenient place to rest and refuel with lunch. Bathrooms are nearby.

When you're ready to continue, backtrack 25 yards from the picnic area where you'll notice a small path veering left into the woods. This path, a section of the Cataract Trail, leads through dense fern and moss covered woods paralleling Cataract Stream. Stay left until you reach a "trail reroute." Designed to prevent trail erosion, these reroutes are clearly marked and comprehensive.

Cataract Trail ends at Rock Springs, a rest stop with picnic tables and bathrooms. Exit the parking lot and head left on Ridgecrest Boulevard. The Old Mine trail head is 20 yards ahead on the opposite side of the road.

Beginning the final leg of today's walk, ascend the fire road and take the first right hand fork. On the left you'll see the famous San Quentin Penitentiary. The Pacific is on your right. Beginning your descent you'll approach a magnificent 180-degree panorama including the Pacific, Marin Headlands, Golden Gate Bridge, San Francisco, the East and North Bay. You'll want to follow the markers leading towards Pantoll. Eventually, with a switchback descent, you'll come to a paved road and turn right. This leads back to the Pantoll Ranger Station and marks the end of your walk.

Walk #4: Point Reyes National Seashore - Coast Trail from Palomarin Parking Lot to Pelican Lake

Walking Easy Time
5 hours

Voted one of the ten best National Seashores in the United States by *Audubon* magazine, and rated the number one Bay Area park by the *San Francisco Chronicle*, Point Reyes National Seashore is understandably the pride of the North Bay. Situated just west of the San Andreas Fault, miles of rugged coastline, coniferous forests, and lowland chaparral areas provide a relatively undisturbed and protected habitat for a diverse range of native flora and fauna.

This 65,000-acre park is huge, and today's walk, which begins at the Palomarin area on the southern end of the park, explores just one fragment of its vastness.

If there is time, you may consider driving north to Olema where you'll find the main entrance and visitor center. Here you can learn more about this fascinating region before venturing into its rich wilderness.

Visitors should keep in mind that this area is often chilly and strong winds are common. Dress accordingly.

Directions: Take the State Highway 1 exit off Highway 101 in Marin County, and head northwest toward Stinson Beach. Pass Stinson and continue four and a half miles along the eastern shore of the Bolinas Lagoon. Upon reaching the tip of the lagoon keep a lookout for the Bolinas-Olema Road on the left. It takes you back along the other side of the Lagoon toward Bolinas. Before reaching the town center, turn right on Mesa Road. After two and a quarter miles the road becomes gravel and dead ends at the Palomarin parking lot and Coast trailhead.

The Coast Trail extends for 13 miles along the southern length of Point Reyes National Seashore. Today's walk will cover only three and a half of those miles (one way) but lends an authentic taste for this rugged wilderness. Paralleling the shoreline, the Coast Trail leads along cliff tops and lake shores, through eucalyptus and pine groves. It also crosses chaparral and meadowlands, and provides some of northern California's most spectacular seascapes.

Consider making this an afternoon walk since the bluffs are often shrouded in morning fog. There are no picnic facilities and primitive bathrooms are situated near the parking lot. Bring a picnic blanket and packed snack to feast upon midway, overlooking scenic Pelican Lake.

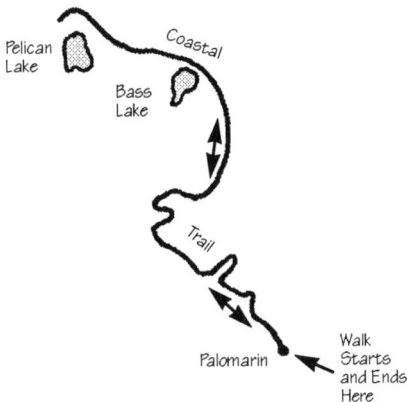

Start: Beginning at the far end of the Palomarin parking lot, the Coast Trail forges north through an extended eucalyptus wold before ascending grass-lined seaside cliffs overlooking the Pacific. Vistas north and south offer outstanding coastal views of the rugged shoreline.

Heading east and inland toward a more wooded, riparian region requires a slight ascent through a narrow, rocky ravine. Rocks are loose, so watch your footing. As the trail levels off near the top, turn left at the fork, remaining on Coast Trail.

Continue through serene meadowlands where a scenic pond rests peacefully on your left. The pathway narrows, entering a region of soft chaparral, coastal sagebrush, and coyote brush. Soon you'll reach a clearing where below you on the left is verdant Bass Lake. Look for waterfowl feeding here and, in the warm summer months, enjoy a swim.

Pass through a lush area forested with Douglas firs before reaching the next trail marker. Continue straight ahead at the junction and after half a mile, Pelican Lake shimmers in the distance. Proceed to the northern side of the lake and follow the narrow path which breaks left off the main trail.

After you've enjoyed a leisurely meal overlooking the lake, begin your return, backtracking along the same beautiful trail.

Walk #5: Angel Island State Park - Northridge Trail to Sunset Trail

Walking Easy Time
2½ hours

Angel Island may not be the best known spot in San Francisco Bay, but it is certainly the most inviting. The name is drawn from its Spanish christening, *Isla de Los Angeles*. Climbing up from this isle's sandy coves, you can explore oak woodlands and groves of eucalyptus and Australian tea trees.

The island's peak, 750-foot Mount Livermore, is named for the Marin County conservationist, Caroline Livermore, who led the transformation of this surplus military site into a State Park in 1954. Some people believe she is the island's real angel.

Long before becoming a park, the island was used for hunting purposes by Marin's Coast Miwoks who routinely paddled over from the mainland on tule reed boats. When Spanish explorers first arrived in the late 1700s, Lt. Juan Manuel de Ayala anchored his ship, the *San Carlos*, in today's Ayala Cove. The island became a Spanish cattle ranch in 1837.

After California achieved Statehood in 1850 the island became a Federal outpost. Over the next century it served as a military base, quarantine station, and immigration station. Today, many of the park's forts and garrison's remain as a memorial to that early era.

Directions: Traveling by ferry is your only access to Angel Island State Park. You have several options depending on where you're based. From San Francisco's Pier 43 ½ at Fisherman's Wharf take the **Red and White Fleet.** Call 1-800-BAY CRUISE for schedule and fare information. The short voyage from Tiburon runs more frequently. It is operated by the **Angel Island State Park Ferry Company.** Information may be obtained by calling (415) 435-2131.

This loop leads walkers up through a densely forested region of oak and bay laurel trees toward panoramic summit views of the Bay Area. The second (western) leg descends through isolated clearings before switchbacking towards Ayala Cove. Restrooms and picnic facilities are located in Ayala Cove and near the summit.

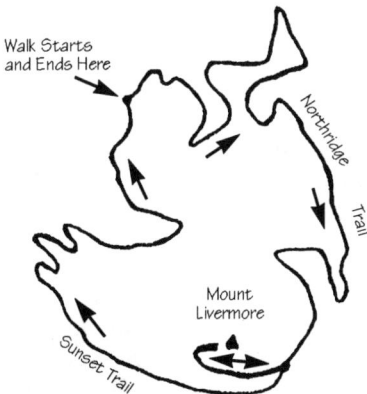

Walk Starts
and Ends Here

Northridge Trail

Mount
Livermore

Sunset Trail

Start: After leaving the ferry in Ayala Cove, exit the docks and veer left of the restrooms and island snack bar toward Northridge Trail. Begin a steeply graded ascent that gradually becomes a wooden stairway before leveling off. Enjoy vistas of Ayala Cove and the cities of Belvedere and Tiburon across Raccoon Strait.

Picnic tables shaded by coast live oak and fragrant bay laurel trees are ideal places for a rest or lunch.

Northridge Trail continues its ascent toward Mount Livermore after crossing Perimeter Road. A gentler incline leads through more oak woodlands and delicate California hazelnut trees. Emerging from tree cover, the footpath opens onto a 20-yard clearing with spectacular views of Mount Tamalpais. Here, you'll pass through an elfin forest colored by manzanita, coyote brush, and chamise.

Ascend the island's wooded east side to another clearing where you'll have your first glimpse of the spectacular San Francisco skyline across the Bay. Further on, Northridge Trail intersects a paved path leading right towards the peak. There's a restroom at this intersection, along with a sign about the park's attempt to restore Angel Island's native vegetation.

Take the short, steep climb to Mount Livermore's summit to enjoy 360-degree panoramic views of the entire region. Here, informative signposts detail distant sights and picnic tables spot the ridge top.

When you're ready to descend, return along Sunset Trail which picks up where Northridge Trail left off. This trail traverses the island's western ridge. Very different from the forested, northeastern side, this part of the island is open and grassy. Views of the Golden Gate are magnificent. Cross paved Perimeter Road to begin your gradual descent through the oak forests on the island's north face. A lengthy series of switchbacks exits onto a paved road where your choice of several paths leads back to Ayala Cove.

Walk #6: Jack London State Historic Park - Lake Trail to Mountain Trail to Upper Fallen Bridge Trail to Fallen Bridge Trail to Upper Lake Trail to Lake Spur and back along Lake Trail.

Walking Easy Time
2½ hours

Just west of downtown Glen Ellen, 800 acres of mixed ever-green forests, grassy meadows, historic structures, hiking, and riding trails add up to one of the most enjoyable parks in North-ern California. They were once the domain of legendary writer, Jack London. Drawn to this beautiful terrain in 1905, London began farming the land and building a home for himself and his wife Charmain.

Today visitors can view London's cottage, explore remnants of an old winery scattered around Beauty Ranch, tour the house of Happy Walls, and hike to the impressive foundation of Wolf House, the mansion that burnt to the ground a month before he and his wife were to move in.

London died in 1916, and years later the state of Califor-nia acquired much of the original 1,400 acres along with the House of Happy Walls, the stone building constructed by Lon-don's wife after his death. Today it serves as a commemorative museum.

Plan to spend at least half a day at Jack London State His-toric Park. In addition to exploring Beauty Ranch, the museum, and Wolf House, today's walk will guide you beyond idyllic Bath-house Lake, deep into the wilderness London loved.

Directions: Head west on Arnold Drive off State Highway 12 in Sonoma County. As Arnold Drive heads through the center of Glen Ellen it veers sharply west. Continue west on London Ranch Road until you reach the park entrance.

Today's hike offers *Easy Walkers* a chance to enjoy the land that captivated and inspired Jack London. Lake Trail is a mile in length and climbs towards the swimming hole, engi-neered by London, where he often entertained guests with bar-becues and horseback rides. Picnic tables dotting the shoreline make this a pleasant spot for lunch.

You can shorten today's planned walk by returning here, or continue for another hour and a half and tour the nether mead-ows and woodlands.

Start: Beginning in the right hand parking lot behind the entrance kiosk, make your way past the eucalyptus grove and open picnic area to the buildings of Beauty Ranch on your left. Some of these buildings, such as the cottage where he spent much of his time writing, London built himself. Others are rem-nants of the late 19th-century Kohler & Frohling winery which

London converted to farming use after purchasing the property.

After you've had a chance to tour the ranch, bear right on Lake Trail rimming the privately owned vineyards. This path remains level, passing blackberry bushes before reaching the junction at the far side of the vineyard. Here, you have the option of taking the Service Road or the densely forested Lake Trail to Bathhouse Lake. We urge you to head right, and ascend into the cool, shady forest of towering redwoods, delicate hazelnut and maple trees, tanbark oak, and Douglas firs.

The short woodland journey leads to London's scenic swimming hole—half its original size because of sediment and thick sedge growth along the pond's rim. The bathhouse where guests could shower and change is located to the right and the restroom is up ahead on your left. Several shaded picnic tables make this a pleasant lunching spot.

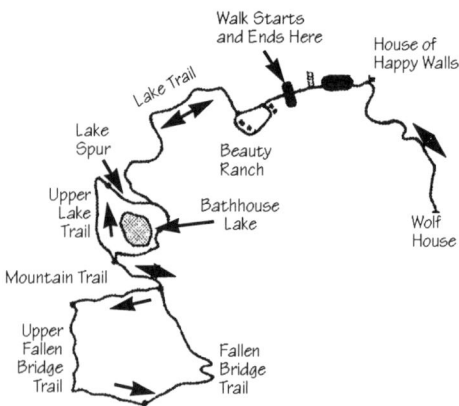

To head further into the heart of London's estate toward Sonoma Mountain, follow Mountain Trail. It begins near the restroom and briefly traverses the lake's southern section. Veering sharply left at the first intersection, Mountain Trail ascends past stands of oak and fragrant bay laurel trees, and exits onto Mays Clearing and Vista Point.

Proceed on Mountain Trail for a quarter of a mile and then turn left on Upper Fallen Bridge Trail. Firs and madrones brighten the beginning of this trail which leads to Woodcutter's Meadow. Patches of manzanita, coyote brush, oak scrub, and other chaparral dot the grassy clearing just as the footpath begins its descent into the cool, lush canyon carved by North Asbury Creek. Portions of this trail descend steeply. Use caution as you head downhill.

Nearing the bottom, cross left over the wooden footbridge and continue your trek along the other side, parallel to the creek. Now on Fallen Bridge Trail, the path gradually breaks from the moist riparian environment, traverses a chaparral laden landscape, and heads up through Mays Clearing to Vista Point again.

Retrace Mountain Trail as if heading back toward the lake. When Mountain Trail descends right, however, proceed straight on Upper Lake Trail. Lake Spur, after a quarter of a mile, provides a short cut to Lake Trail which leads back to Beauty Ranch.

* * *

A visit to the House of Happy Walls, the park's museum, is a must before leaving Jack London State Historic Park. Inside, you'll find exhibits of London's books, journals, and nautical equipment from his *Snark* journeys. Also here are mementos from his foreign journeys as a war correspondent, architectural plans for the magnificent Wolf House, original manuscripts, and family artifacts gracing period rooms.

Also a must is the short trek down to the remains of London's Wolf House, the $80,000 dream home destroyed in a mysterious fire only a month before the Londons were scheduled to move in. Be sure to keep an eye out for rattlesnakes on this trail. Enjoy them at a safe distance. This route is just a little over half a mile and leads through a forest of Douglas firs, manzanita, and madrones.

Walk #7: Annadel State Park - Lower Steve's Trail to Warren Richardson Trail

Walking Easy Time
2½ hours

Annadel State Park, hunting grounds for the southern Wappo and Pomo Indian Tribes before becoming a ranching enclave for Spanish and American settlers, is now a 5,000-acre recreational paradise. Thirty-six miles of trails explore this historic region rich in scenery and delightfully uncrowded.

Named "Annie's Dell" after Anne Hutchinson, the granddaughter of one of the region's prominent ranchers, this area was a major source of obsidian used by Native Americans to make tools and weapons. At the turn of the century, quarrying began here for the cobblestone used to pave the streets of San Francisco.

Directions: Heading north on State Highway 12, turn left on Los Alamos Road just past the small community of Oakmont. At the first stop sign turn right on Melita Road which immediately veers left, becoming Montgomery Drive. Turn left onto Channel Drive after half a mile. Drive for almost two miles and stop at the ranger station to pay for parking. Here you can also purchase a map for an additional charge. The parking lot is another mile further on where the paved road dead ends and the trails begin.

A soft trek to Lake Islanjo and back, this easy walk with gentle grades winds through cool redwoods, oak woodlands, and open meadows. Bathrooms are available in the parking lot at the start of the walk and midway, near the lake. Picnic tables are located lake side and spread out along Warren Richardson Trail.

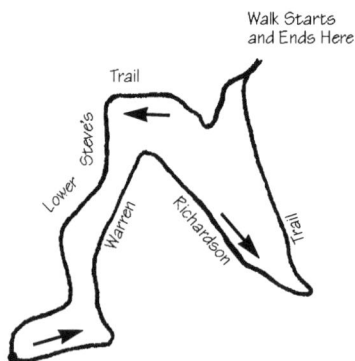

Walk Starts and Ends Here

Trail

Lower Steve's

Warren

Richardson

Trail

Start: At the far end of the parking lot *Easy Walkers* will find a small spur switchback, lined with fragrant bay laurels, leading up to the marker for Lower Steve's Trail.

You'll ascend gradually through a partial redwood stand mixed with madrones and stately firs. The fern-lined trail levels onto a flat, open meadowland spotted with coast live and valley oak trees. In springtime yellow globe lilies brighten the landscape.

Remaining on Lower Steve's, begin your descent past oak trees and chaparral to Lake Islanjo. The lake appears below while Bennett Mountain looms loftily in the distance. Just beyond the oaks extends another large meadow bordering the lake. Here, birds rummaging in the scrub along the path penetrate the silence; and if you're lucky, as we were, you may see uninhibited deer foraging not far from the footpath.

Upon reaching the junction with Warren Richardson Trail near the base of Lake Ilsanjo, bear left.

If you're feeling good and have time, enjoy the two-mile trail network circling the lake. You may wish to relax near the shore of Ilsanjo, well stocked with black bass and blue gill. Look for the lone picnic table resting in the shade of a sprawling oak, 100 yards to the right of the junction. Laced with tall sedges and cattails, the lake's edge is not far from this enclave. Restrooms are positioned in either direction around the lake.

Today's return trek is along the wider, multi-purpose Warren Richardson Trail. Beginning with an ascent, this trail, initially lined with tall oaks and yellow star thistle, heads eastward. The path wends through dry, chaparral lined clearings with scattered madrones and then enters the cool haven of coast redwoods. Several picnic tables (at the Louis Trail junction, near the water tank, and at the junction with Two Quarry Trail) line this trail if you prefer to lunch later.

The second half of the Warren Richardson Trail completes its descent through towering redwoods before reaching Two Quarry Trail. At this junction bear right (sharply). The trail, which leads back to the parking lot, is wide and at times offers vistas of the eastern valley and opposite range.

You'll pass once again, on your left, the Lower Steve's trailhead. Just beyond this point, veer right and descend the narrow spur trail leading to the lot.

Walk #8: Armstrong Redwoods State Reserve - East Ridge Trail to Pioneer Trail to Discovery Trail and back on Pioneer Trail

Walking Easy Time
2½ hours

Approximately 60 miles north of San Francisco, Armstrong Redwoods State Reserve rests snugly in the far regions of Sonoma County. The virgin redwoods are a monument to one man's understanding and initiative. He is Colonel James A. Armstrong, a one-time logger who valued the beauty of the forest over its utility. In 1870 he set aside this land as a park for others to appreciate and enjoy.

The last remaining old growth forest in Sonoma County, this 728-acre park also hosts several beautiful plant communities which can be explored via trails connecting the Reserve to adjacent Austin Creek State Recreation Area.

At the visitor center take a look at the informative exhibits inside. Of special interest is the chart pinpointing redwood communities around the world, from the Ice Age to modern times. The story is a sad one documenting the importance of preserves like this one.

Directions: To reach the Reserve, located in Guerneville, take U.S. Highway 101 north past Petaluma and exit northwest onto State Highway 116. This scenic route passes through Russian River country and actually crosses the River before reaching Guerneville.

When you reach the town's main junction, drive straight ahead on Armstrong Woods Road. The park is located several miles further ahead. Park in the visitor center parking lot on your right, just before reaching the entrance kiosk.

We've designed today's walk to help visitors enjoy Armstrong's spectacular redwood basin and the mixed wilderness beyond. We also recommend a short detour off Discovery Trail to the Redwood Forest Theater (explained in greater detail below). While restrooms cannot be found along any of the trails, they are located at the visitor center, in the picnic area separating East Ridge from Pioneer Trail, and at the Theater.

Start: Today's walk begins on the right side of the visitor center. A steep, initial ascent along East Ridge Trail makes this leg the most challenging part of the hike. The higher elevation offers *Easy Walkers* a chance to experience the transition from the moist redwood basin into a dryer mixed evergreen forest. It also makes for a pleasant getaway from the tourist crowds who come to the park solely to see the redwoods on the valley floor.

A switchback ascent, where tan bark oaks and Douglas firs are interspersed among the redwoods, leads hikers up along the ridge. As the trail descends, madrones and California bay laurels proliferate.

Fork left after a mile's trek and immediately head left again at the first marker. This half mile spur towards the picnic area, switchbacks down towards the basin and into the heart of redwood country. Here, trunks of massive girth rise steeply, hundreds of feet into the sky.

Exit this trail finding yourself in a small, paved parking area where picnic tables lie shaded along the outskirts. This is an enjoyable place to stop for a snack or lunch before continuing onward.

When ready to progress, head south and out of the lot. Remain on the paved road as it follows along side of Fife Creek, and you'll hook up with Pioneer Trail.

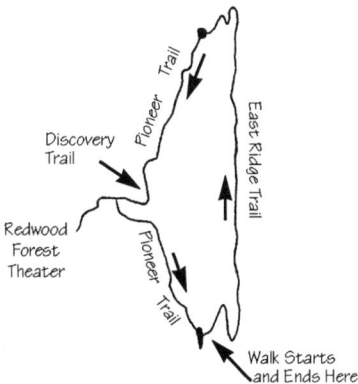

Along with Discovery Trail, this is a popular route made for *Easy Walkers*. This well traveled forest path, part of a self-guided nature trail, is a great place to learn about coast redwoods and their environment. Redwoods thrive in regions such as this, where they are nurtured by moisture received from Northern California's fog belt. They additionally crave rich alluvial soil, dank from winter rains and stream flooding.

Half a mile into Pioneer Trail, at the first marker, turn right onto Discovery Trail. Icicle Tree appears soon after this detour. One of several Discovery Trail highlights, these icicle-like growths, actually dormant buds extending from the tree's trunk, are called burls. At one time this tree held many icicle burls. Sadly most have been removed over the years by vandals.

Bracken and sword fern, as well as redwood sorrel (the shamrock-like clovers), line the forest bed and help retain the soil's moisture.

Eventually you'll arrive at Colonel Armstrong Tree. Named after the man responsible for preserving the area, this natural wonder is an estimated 1,400 years old and ranks second among the Reserve's tallest trees at 308 feet.

A short, half-mile detour to the Redwood Forest Theater is accessible from this point and well worth a visit. Once used for staged artistic events, this serene area is an inviting place for a quiet rest. You may also choose to picnic here.

Returning to Discovery Trail, your path heads southeast and merges once again with Pioneer Trail before crossing a service road. In the short remaining distance you'll tread a path of wonderfully scented, crushed California bay laurel leaves and arrive at the reserve's tallest tree. Not quite as old as Colonel Armstrong, Parson Jones Tree is a full two feet taller at 310 feet.

Your return to the visitor center from this point is an easy southern stroll along the service road.

Walk #9: Sugarloaf Ridge State Park - Lower Bald Mountain Trail to Bald Mountain Trail to Vista Trail to Grey Pine Trail to Hillside Trail to Creekside Nature Trail

Walking Easy Time
3 hours

Twenty-one miles of trails lace 2,700 acres of intriguing wilderness embraced by Sugarloaf Ridge State Park. Named for Mountain peaks which rim the park and resemble "sugar loafs" sold by grocers before modern packaging, this State Park is located just north of Kenwood in the Mayacamas Mountains straddling Sonoma and Napa counties.

Sugarloaf sheltered an entire Wappo Indian village prior to the arrival of Spanish settlers in the early 1800s. In the latter half of the century American settlers farmed the land which came under the ownership of "gentlemen farmers." They spent most of their time in San Francisco while others tilled the land. The state purchased the property in 1920, and 45 years later opened Sugarloaf to the public as part of the California State Park system.

Directions: Traveling north on State Highway 12, turn right on Adobe Canyon Road several miles after passing through Kenwood. You will see a sign for the park just before the turnoff. Continue on Adobe Canyon Road for several miles before reaching the park.

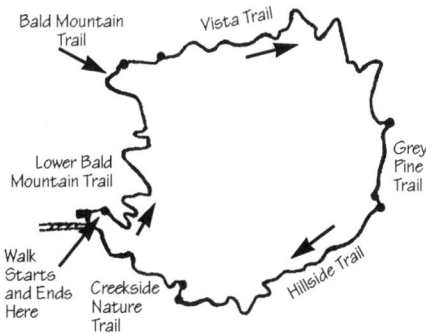

Roughly divided into three sections, the first third of today's hike climbs toward the summit of Bald Mountain. The second slowly traverses an open clearing and winds downward, capturing magnificent views of the peaks and valley below. The final leg leisurely meanders through the valley.

The best time for walking Sugarloaf Ridge State Park is in the early morning, when the sun slowly warms the mist away and you are likely to spot black tailed deer, raccoons, and grey squirrels. Only the latter half of Hillside Trail offers picnic facilities.

You will find both restroom and picnic facilities at park headquarters, near the parking lot and campgrounds.

Start: On the east side of the parking lot you'll find a trail-head for two routes—Lower Bald Mountain Trail, and the small spur trail leading to the Bay Area Ridge Trail. Several yards further on, at the next post, bear right, following the brown arrow, and begin your trek towards the summit of Bald Mountain.

This footpath initially leads through thick grasslands, brightened by yellow star thistle in late spring and summer. A gradual ascent passes through oak clusters, Douglas firs, and chaparral patches as it winds up into a dense grove of valley and coast live oak, complemented by colorful madrones. The trail exits onto a clearing, lined with a handsome elfin forest where coyote brush, manzanita, wine bush, and chamise create a colorful patchwork.

Upon reaching the paved Bald Mountain Trail, veer right, and continue on a long, quarter-of-a-mile, uphill stretch.

You won't miss Vista Trail, which leads right and descends quickly through a wooded patch of big leaf maples. The fern-lined floor is laced by a small tributary. This trail continues to a grassy ridge offering excellent views of Sugarloaf Ridge and the miniature valley below.

After traversing the ridge for a half a mile veer inland and enter a thick madrone and oak woodland. Be cautious of the steep descent.

After passing through several small meadows, look for Grey Pine Trail where you'll bear right, and parallel one of the many tributaries supplying Sonoma Creek. A riparian environment of red alders and big leaf maples—the largest in California—offers a cool alternative to the dryer woodlands above.

Continue on Grey Pine Trail to Sonoma Creek. After crossing Sonoma Creek turn left at the intersection and return along Hillside Trail.

This path traverses the length of the Valley near the base of Sugarloaf Ridge. Spotted with mushrooming oak trees, this wide trail is a hiker's delight, especially in late summer when you can nibble on blackberries from bushes lining the path.

A picnic table sits on a slight promontory, offering clear views of Bald Mountain. There is also a water fountain to quench your thirst.

After a short descent, turn right at the first fork and left at the second. The final half mile of today's walk, along Creekside

Nature Trail, crosses Sonoma Creek. You'll enjoy the stream-side environment of willows, maples, Oregon ash, snow and white berries before veering right, away from the campground, to the parking lot.

Walks #10 & 11: Bothe-Napa Valley State Park

The Wappo Indians were the first to explore this volcanic region now known as Bothe-Napa Valley State Park. They were the first to hunt its densely forested northern slopes, and live off the earth along with coyotes, deer, gray squirrels, and spotted owls.

During the Spanish and Mexican period the land was given to Dr. Edward Bale, an English ship surgeon who became a Mexican citizen after marrying Captain Salvador Vallejo's niece in 1839.

After Bale's death, the land passed through many hands, most notably the Hitchcocks, a prominent San Francisco family, and Reinhold Bothe, who tried his hand at running a campground.

The state acquired the land in 1960 after Bothe's death and has worked on preserving this beautiful region ever since.

Two agreeable walks capture the essence of this unique area. The climb to Coyote Peak offers broad views of the valley basin and vineyards below. History Trail, connecting Bothe-Napa Valley to Bale Grist Mill State Park, passes through some of the valley's most important historic sites.

Both of these walks can be completed the same day. Plan on picnicking between the two or, if you prefer, arrange half day walks on alternate days while incorporating visits to Napa's famous wineries.

Directions: Located in the heart of Napa Valley, the park lies on the western side of State Highway 29 between St. Helena and Calistoga. You'll want to park in the Horse Trailer area—the trailhead for today's walks. There is a small parking fee as well as an additional charge for a park map.

Walk #10: Coyote Peak Trail

Walking Easy Time
2½ hours

Climbing to an elevation of 1,170 feet, this walk is a bit of a challenge but well worth the effort. It leads to the top of Coyote Peak which offers a great view of the valley below where handsome vineyards form a natural patchwork framed by distant mountains.

Because of the moderately strenuous climb and summer temperatures much warmer than San Francisco's, this is definitely an early morning walk.

There are no bathroom or picnic facilities on the trail. Plan on lunching when you return to the Horse Trailer area where picnic tables and restrooms are located nearby.

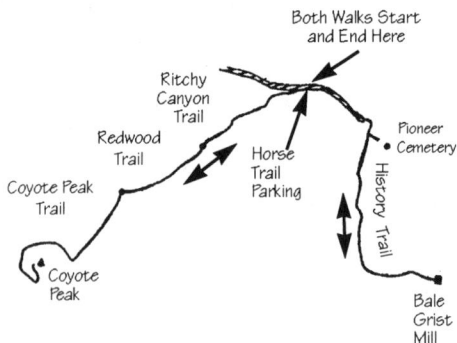

Start: At the north end of the parking area is a sign for Ritchie Canyon Trail. This initial spur path crosses a paved road and heads past the park's employee residence before merging with the main trail. The wider trail, following the southern bank of Ritchie Creek, offers a level stroll through shady coast redwoods and Douglas firs. Before Ritchie Trail crosses the creek towards the campground, veer left onto Redwood Trail.

This leg parallels the creek, heading further into the canyon depths where you'll see big leaf maple and bay laurel trees.

Coyote Peak Trail bears left off Redwood Trail. This intersection is marked by several large patches of manzanita with twisting maroon trunks coloring the evergreen forest.

Leaving Ritchie Creek, this trail climbs up the mountain towards its summit. Near the top, orange madrones share the steep mountainside with manzanita, chamise, and coyote brush. Eventually the footpath opens and views extend clear across the canyon to the opposite ridge.

Here, follow the rocky path breaking left, away from the main trail toward the peak. There is plenty of shade at the very top where you can relax and enjoy the beautiful scenery below. When you're ready to return, simply backtrack and make your way down the trail.

Walk #11: History Trail

Walking Easy Time
1½ hours

For those fascinated with the past, this trail takes walkers on a journey to historic Napa sites. An out and back hike, extending between Bothe-Napa Valley and Bale Grist Mill state parks, this walk, shorter and less challenging than Coyote Peak Trail, makes for a pleasant afternoon stroll.

Start: The trailhead is located at the southern end of the paved road, beyond the picnic area. Near the start you'll approach Pioneer Cemetery, located on the site of Napa's first chapel.

Your route climbs through oak woodlands, colorfully accented with madrones. The path levels off in dry grassland, spotted with manzanita and scrub oak, before beginning its slow descent toward Bale Grist Mill State Historic Park.

Along the way take the short detour to the site of Mill Pond which once fed the Bale Grist Mill. The mill and water wheel replica are only a short distance away.

Your fee into Bothe-Napa Valley State Park provides free access into the mill, where you will find informative exhibits on the history of this mill, constructed in the early 1840s by Edward Turner Bale.

THE EAST BAY

Just minutes from the city, the East Bay is the home of a famous university, Jack London's birthplace, and a multicultural community famous for its educative life, restaurants, and handsome architecture.

Originally known as "Contra Costa," or the "other coast," the singular East Bay region was partitioned in 1853 to include Alameda County. Flatlands and marshes near the Bay, hillside regions shaded by Eucalyptus, pastoral valleys, and the slopes of Mount Diablo make this diverse area an attractive place to work and play.

A multicultural hub, the East Bay is a place where you can enjoy Afghan cuisine, Peruvian street music, African American theater, and shop for Nabokov novels in Russian in a single day. No matter what your roots, you'll always feel at home here.

The region's most intriguing cultural asset is the University of California. Simply frequent any of the nearby cafes along Bancroft Way or Telegraph Avenue and eavesdrop on heated conversations ranging from gender equality to global economics.

The site of many revolutions, Berkeley remains, in many ways, a 60's cultural shrine. Walk down Telegraph Avenue from the University campus to People's Park, and you'll find today's undergraduates, yesterday's hippies, the homeless, a wide array of wannabes, and crusaders fighting for causes that are up to the minute and in some cases hopelessly obsolete.

Sitting just south is Berkeley's big sibling and other major East Bay neighborhood, Oakland. Among the city's architectural landmarks are the Grand Lake and Paramount theaters, the Oakland Museum, and apartment houses surrounding picturesque Lake Merritt in the heart of downtown Oakland.

The parklands in Alameda and Contra Costa County, found along the shore and up in the wooded hills, are also inviting.

The East Bay hills, dividing the urban shoreline region from the inland suburban communities of Lafayette, Walnut Creek, and Concord, are this region's primary wilderness. These parklands are maintained and preserved by the East Bay Regional Park District (EBRPD). Other popular hiking spots are found on the slopes of Mount Diablo and wilderness areas to the south.

Alameda and Contra Costa's first inhabitants were sub-tribes of the Ohlone and Miwok Indians, such as the Huchiun, Yrgin, Karkins, or Saclan. After thousands of years their stable and rhythmic life as hunters, gatherers, and fishermen came to and end with the 1769 "discovery" of the Bay Area by the Portola Expedition.

Religious conversion, abuse, and disease depleted the existing tribes on the eastern shore. Converted to Christianity, abused, and ultimately devastated by white man's diseases, the tribes quickly lost control of the region.

By the late 18th century, the Spanish *Mission de San Jose* governed this rich grazing land. Before the Spanish arrived, these hillsides were carpeted with "bunch" or perennial grasses which were suited to the strong heat accompanying long summer months. The new settlers planted seasonal grass seeds which quickly changed the region's appearance.

The first Spanish inhabitants arrived in 1820 when Luis Maria Peralta was deeded the region in exchange for his years of military service. Several years later, after the Mexican Rebellion, this 47,000-acre deed was regranted to him by the Mexican Government. Later, Peralta divided his land, known as *Rancho San Antonio*, between his four sons.

Like the Indians before him, Peralta and his descendants were victimized by a new generation of settlers. When the Gold Rush hit in 1849, hoards of white settlers assumed control of the region. Settlers had no regard for the Treaty of Guadalupe Hidalgo which gave Mexicans this abundant region.

Most of the 49'ers were anchored in San Francisco, but the East Bay, boasting one route to the mines, also had a number of settlements. Oakland's inland redwoods, standing up to 300 feet tall, became navigational landmarks for ships entering the Bay. They were also a major resource for lumbermen supplying San Francisco. By 1860 these redwood forests were history. Commercial loggers ignored the fact that they had no legal claim to the land of Jose Vincent Peralta, who inherited the region which now embraces Oakland. When California was admitted to the United States as a state in 1850 the plight of Spanish and Mexican rancheros worsened.

Unable to keep up with levied property taxes and unwilling to take part in the mining frenzy, the Peralta family bartered away most of their holdings.

White settlers purchased the Peralta's land for cattle grazing. They were joined by western pioneers and immigrants. Frustrated with mining, they built homes along the Bay's eastern shore. New ferry ports served these settlers and entrepreneurs built grist mills to support emerging communities.

San Francisco's checkered reputation was also a factor in the East Bay's population growth. The men who dominated San Francisco (women were a distinct minority) added new meaning to the term "wild west." San Francisco's Barbary Coast was a mecca for drugs, liquor, prostitution, and gun play. Miners and pioneers who brought their wives and families west wanted a safe and sane lifestyle that would parallel the eastern decency they left behind. They found that balance in the East Bay where churches and schools were quickly built across the region.

Certainly the most prestigious was the University of California. Initially located in Oakland, it was moved to the base of the Berkeley hills.

As Oakland and Berkeley grew, farsighted civic leaders began taking steps to preserve the surrounding wilderness.

Toward the end of the 19th century, community leaders, landscape architect Frederick Law Olmsted, and other preservationists suggested protecting East Bay lands along the shoreline. Their suggestions went unheeded as competing water companies started purchasing open space, building ditches, and damming canyons for future watershed land.

By the 1920s most of these independent companies had merged under the control of the East Bay Municipal Water District (EBMUD). Because water was now being routed from the Sierra there was little need for 10,000 acres of watershed land in the East Bay. At the same time urban growth was booming and hungry developers were eager to acquire and convert the unwanted cashement basins.

As developers began eyeing the watershed wilderness, public spirited residents moved decisively. The University and community leaders, such as Robert Sibley and Major Charles Lee
Tilden, established the East Bay Regional Park Association, and
urged EBMUD to open up the land. An Association was created to manage the land and was funded in 1934 by an Alameda
County tax increase. Even in the midst of the depression, residents were eager to finance new parklands and prevent developers from taking away their wilderness.

In 1936, with personal donations and money the district
had acquired from the new tax, three park areas totaling 2,166
acres were purchased from EBMUD.

Tilden Park, the first established after the founding of the
park district, was largely a product of the depression era. Financed
via federal funds, the park also benefited from the Works Project Administration (WPA), the Public Works Administration
(PWA), and the Civilian Conservation Corps (CCC). These groups
constructed roads, cleared picnic sites, hiking, and equestrian
trails, and built tables, playing fields, and the self-supporting golf
course in Tilden Regional Park.

The park district continued to grow and in 1964 Contra
Costa County joined the EBRPD. Between 1950 and 1967 the
district quadrupled to 22,000 acres in 20 parks.

Today urbanization remains a problem as developers covet
wilderness areas adjacent to the parks.

The Feel of Walks in the East Bay

When explorers first sighted the Bay's eastern shore they
saw miles of oak groves extending inland. While Oakland's forests
have given way to development, it's still possible to find wilderness nearby. Open grasslands, scattered oak groves, and elfin
forests make the parkland a delightful spot for a day's outing.

Transportation to the East Bay

AC Transit offers bus service from the San Francisco Bus
Terminal to the East Bay. For a faster, smoother ride, BART
transports visitors from downtown San Francisco to both Oak-

land and Berkeley locations as well as cities further inland such as Orinda, Lafayette, Walnut Creek, Pleasant Hill, and Concord.

Drivers coming from San Francisco will initially want to take I-80 over the Bay Bridge. To reach Berkeley remain on I-80 as it travels northeast and exit onto University Avenue which leads to the UC campus and the Berkeley hills. Turning right on Shattuck Avenue several blocks south of the campus, takes you to downtown Berkeley.

To reach downtown Oakland by car, take I-580 east from the Bay Bridge toll plaza and continue south on I-980. There are three downtown Oakland exits off Interstate 980 at 19th, 14th, or 12th streets.

Activities and Excursions in the East Bay

Like San Francisco, the East Bay blends urban culture with an enticing wilderness at its doorstep. The visitor has plenty of options depending on his or her mood. The following section describes alternative activities and excursions for *Easy Walkers*. Most of the noteworthy sights in the East Bay center around Berkeley and Oakland.

1. University of California at Berkeley. No trip to the East Bay is complete without a visit to *the* University of California. Founded in 1870, this campus has become one of the world's great institutions of learning. The renowned faculty, including nine Nobel laureates, teaches over 30,000 students.

📝 **HINT: Parking around the campus and downtown Berkeley is scarce; much of it metered or by permit only. If you drive, consider parking in a garage near campus. Inexpensive Sather Gate Garage, located on Durant Avenue, between Dana Street and Telegraph Avenue is only a block from campus. Park downtown at 2025 Center Street.**

Many of Berkeley's leading sights are associated with the University. **Sproul Plaza**, located just beyond the main entrance to the campus at Telegraph Avenue and Bancroft Way, is the city's Hyde Park corner—an open forum for every corner of the political spectrum.

Protests, announced in the school's newspaper, *The Daily California*, are staged here regularly during the school year. Sitting in the plaza, lunch in hand, and watching the protesters, students, and Berkeley eccentrics stroll by, can make for a very entertaining and sometimes enlightening afternoon.

Campus tours are available daily but you can very easily improvise your own, leisurely enjoying Berkeley's great architectural heritage. In 1896 Bernard Maybeck, then a lecturer in architecture at the University, organized a campus design competition with funding from Phoebe Apperson Hearst. Henri Jean Emile Bérnard won the contest and collected his prize money, but failed to complete the job.

Maybeck then brought in a finalist, John Galen Howard, to oversee campus design. Many of the more spectacular buildings on campus are the product of Howard's tenure as supervising architect. Buildings by other notable architects such as Julia Morgan and Maybeck are campus landmarks.

Even before the University opened its classrooms to students two buildings were erected, North Hall and South Hall. The oldest building still on campus, constructed in 1873, **South Hall** was designed by the University's first official architect, David Farquharson. This graceful brick structure, located southwest of the Campanile, was recently renovated to prevent earthquake damage.

The **Hearst Mining Building** (1907), on the northeast side of the campus is John Galen Howard's beautiful Beaux Arts masterpiece.

Modeled after the Greek Theatre in Epidaurus, **Hearst Greek Theatre** (1903) was designed by California's preeminent woman architect, Julia Morgan.

The University's main book repository, **Doe Library** (1917) is the largest library in the western United, and another Howard design. Take a peek at the scholarly reference room upstairs or the Morrison Memorial Library, a cozy downstairs reading room.

The popular 307-foot-high **Campanile** (1914) was modeled after the tower at Venice's Plaza San Marco. A grand bell carillon plays daily. You can ride to the top for only 50 cents.

Next head south toward the grassy expanse on the other side of Strawberry Creek known as Faculty Glade. On the eastern rim of the Glade is the **Faculty Club**, a rustic structure, designed by Maybeck, where visiting professors reside and events are staged.

The first of its kind, **Hearst Gymnasium for Women** (1927), designed by Julia Morgan, is a beautiful mazelike structure with several pools, including one on the roof.

> ☞ HINT: The University's visitor center, which organizes tours and provides information, is located off campus in 101 University Hall, 2200 University Avenue; (510) 642-5215.

2. Phoebe Apperson Hearst Museum of Anthropology. (Open 10 to 4:30 Monday through Friday; noon to 4:30 Saturday and Sunday; (510) 643-7648.) Formerly known as the Robert H. Lowie Museum, this research facility houses over 500,000 items from around the world ranging from California ethnography and human osteology to Oceanian archaeology.

Directions: Located in 103 Kroeber Hall on the UC Berkeley Campus at the corner of Bancroft Way and College Avenue.

3. University Art Museum. (Open 11 to 5 Wednesday through Sunday; (510) 642-0808.) Eleven galleries feature world class art as well as student exhibits. An impressive permanent collection includes works by Picasso, Cezanne, Rembrant, Miro, Hoffman, and others.

The **Pacific Film Archive**, featuring rare cinematic works, a comprehensive bookstore, and comfortable cafe, is also housed in this Mario J. Campi designed structure.

Directions: Located across the street from the UC Berkeley Campus at 2626 Bancroft Way.

4. University of California Botanical Garden. Established in 1891, this is the oldest campus botanical garden in the United States. Thirteen thousand different species represent over a dozen geographic regions. A Tropical House, Fern House, and Desert and Rainforest House harbor the Garden's special collections. Streamside benches are a great place to enjoy this idyllic, peaceful enclave also offering splendid views of the Bay.

Directions: Located just east off Centennial Drive in Strawberry Canyon behind the campus.

5. Lawrence Hall of Science. (Open 10 to 5 daily; (510) 642 5132.) Built in 1968 and named after Nobel-Prize winning scientist Ernest O. Lawrence, children and adults alike love this center featuring a giant fiberglass whale on the plaza. In addition to science exhibits ranging from dinosaurs to space travel, the Lawrence Hall of Science features several labs with hands-on exhibits and do-it-yourself experiments.

Directions: On Centennial Drive in the Berkeley hills above the campus.

6. Rose Garden. Constructed in 1937 this scenic garden was a WPA project designed by Bernard Maybeck. Over 250 varieties of colorful, scented roses are arranged in semicircular tiers while spectacular Golden Gate views compliment the beautiful scene.

Directions: Located on 1300 Euclid Street, north of the UC campus in the Berkeley hills.

7. Botanic Garden. (Open 8:30 to 5 daily; (510) 841-8732.) Manzanita and oak shaded lanes wind through this ten-acre garden which is home to 1,500 species of plants native to California. Split by acreage, each of ten sections represents a different area of the state, ranging from the southeastern desert to the northern Pacific rain forest.

Directions: Located in Tilden Park where Wildcat Canyon Road intersects South Park Road across from the Camp Oaks parking area.

> ☞ **HINT: Pick up a copy of the *Berkeley Insider* which has an updated and monthly listing of cultural events, evening entertainment, and extensive restaurant information. The weekly *Express* also offers free East Bay event information as does *The Daily Californian*. The *Oakland Tribune* is another good resource.**

8. Berkeley Marina. (510) 644-6371. If you're interested in water sports such as fishing, sailing, or wind surfing, stop by the clubs and activity centers in the Berkeley Marina. The Hornblower dining yachts are also entertaining.

If you prefer to be a land lubber, explore one of the parks on this little Peninsula. Parents may want to bring their children to the **Adventure Playground**, a hands on recreation area perfect for building objects with donated materials and tools provided by the park.

North Waterfront Park has turned a former dump into a 90-acre green perfect for kite enthusiasts. **Shorebird Park** is another bayshore site with a small, scenic, wooded area, perfect for picnicking.

At the **Berkeley Pier**, you can fish, watch the windsurfers, and view the sun setting over San Francisco.

The current pier was built in the late 1950s and an observation deck was added in 1972. The original Berkeley Pier, Jacobs Landing, was built in 1853. Another wooden, automobile pier extending three miles into the Bay was constructed in 1926 by the Golden Gate Ferry Company. It served commuters ferrying into the city before the Bay Bridge was built in 1936. Pilings from this structure still jut from the Bay's depths and offer a resting spot for the resident seagulls.

Directions: The Berkeley Marina is located at the western end of University Avenue where it meets Marina Boulevard and Seawall Drive.

9. Jack London Square and Village. Primarily a shopping and dining center, this area has several interesting sights including Jack London's **Yukon Cabin** which is perched just outside of **Heinhold's 1880 "First and Last Chance Saloon"**. This entertaining survivor of the 1906 earthquake, remains in operation with slanted floors warped by the seismic event. It's located at the southern end of the square.

Commemorating London and other Bay Area writers is the **Jack London Museum** (30 Jack London Square, Suite 104) and adjoining bookstore. Upstairs take a peek at the **Ebony Museum of Art** which hosts African American antiquities and always has interesting exhibits.

FDR's floating White House, the *Potomac*, rests lazily in the harbor. This ship was later owned by Elvis Presley and ultimately seized in a drug bust before finally being rescued for posterity by a local preservationist group. On Sunday you can gather fresh fruit, vegetables, baked goods, and flowers from the weekly **Farmer's Market**.

Directions: In Oakland, follow Broadway westward all the way until you reach the Bay.

10. Lake Merritt. This shallow spot was originally named Lake Peralta after the Spanish/Mexican family who first owned this East Bay territory. Locals insisted on renaming it Merritt's Lake after Doctor Samuel Merritt who ingeniously transformed it into a scenic downtown lake in the 1860s. A 155-acre salt water lake, its shoreline extends just over three miles making it a perfect site for jogging or dusk strolls when its "necklace of lights" is illuminated.

Lakeside Park is located on the eastern shore. Within this 122-acre park children enjoy puppet shows and sets at **Children's Playland**, the three-dimensional, nursery rhyme and fairy tale park that inspired Disneyland. (Hours vary so call ahead at 510 452-2259.) Older visitors will appreciate the fragrant **Japanese herb garden,** designed for the visually impaired but open for everyone's enjoyment.

Located on the Lake's western shore is the **Camron-Stanford House** (510 836-1976). Originally built in 1876 and now fully restored, it is the last remaining Victorian house on the lake. Tours are available on Wednesdays and Sundays.

In addition to boat rentals and other water activities centered around the lake, annual events are popular here such as the **Festival-at-the-Lake**—a three day affair, held in early June, with arts and crafts, music, and ethnic eats.

Directions: Located in the heart of Oakland, Lake Merritt is bordered by Grand and Lake Shore avenues and Lakeside Drive.

11. Oakland Museum. (Open 10 to 5 Wednesday through Saturday; noon to 7 Sunday; (510) 238-3401.) Referred to by some as the California Smithsonian, the Oakland Museum catalogs California's history, art, and natural sciences. Four galleries include exhibits ranging from the Ohlone Indians to 20th-century kitchens. Take a break, stepping outdoors where footpaths and fishponds grace the impressive Babylonian style roof gardens.

Directions: Located on 10th and Oak streets in downtown Oakland.

12. Paramount Theater. Erected in the 1930s by Paramount Pictures, this impressive art deco structure is a historic landmark that functions as home to the Oakland Ballet and East Bay Symphony. On Friday evenings, the theater showcases early film classics. Tours of the theater are offered the first and third Saturdays of each month for only a dollar. For more information call (510) 465-6400.

Directions: In downtown Oakland at 2025 Broadway.

13. Grand Lake Theater. A fully renovated 1926 historic landmark, the Grand Lake continues to operate as a movie theater. Pre-show performances on the Wurlitzer Organ are always popular.

Directions: The theater is located at the junction of Grand Avenue and Lake Park near the southeastern shore of Lake Merritt.

14. Oakland Zoo. (Open 10 to 4 daily; (510) 632-9523.) Despite the African lions and 300 other exotic animals found here, this is essentially a small town zoo. With so much space, you won't have to battle the crowds, and it's nice to know the animals have freedom to roam. Adults can do the same if they head over to nearby **Knowland Park** with open hills and shady groves.

Directions: 9777 Golf Links Road off Interstate 580 in the Oakland hills.

15. Dunsmuir House and Gardens. (Open 10 to 4 Tuesday through Thursday; (510) 562-0328.) Fifty-seven rooms grace the interior of this Colonial Revival National Historic Site crowned with a Tiffany-style dome. Outside, is a 40-acre spread of hills and gardens featuring exotic trees and sprawling meadows. Jointly owned with the City of Oakland, Dunsmuir House hosts educational, historical, and cultural events. The Christmas season is the ideal time to visit.

Directions: 2960 Peralta Oaks Court (exiting 106th Avenue off I-580 east, go under the freeway and follow the signs).

Accommodations

Elmwood House Bed and Breakfast - 2609 College Avenue, south of the Berkeley campus; (510) 540-5123 [$65-$90]. Each of the four cozy rooms in this delightful Bed and Breakfast are named after architects (Maybeck, Morgan, Howard, and Seely) that have left their distinctive mark on Berkeley. The least known of the four, Edward Seely, designed this turn-of-the-century, traditional Berkeley Bay brown-shingle house. Rooms are comfortable and the proprietors, John and Steve, offer interesting historical information.

Gramma's Rose Garden Inn - 2740 Telegraph Avenue; (510) 549-2145. A colossal Bed & Breakfast with two landmark mansions and three additional houses set around a garden courtyard, Gramma's also harbors a restaurant and is within walking distance of the University and downtown Berkeley. Rooms, ranging from $85-$150, all have private baths, most have fireplaces. [Proprietor: Kathy Kuhner]

Hillegass House - 2834 Hillegass Avenue, south of the Berkeley campus; (510) 548-5517 [$65-$90]. Located in a peaceful residential neighborhood, this large brown-shingle, turn-of-the-century Bed & Breakfast Inn offers comfortable, spacious rooms decorated with fine antiques and an inviting sauna. Guests are encouraged to make themselves at home in the common rooms and on the outdoor deck. [Proprietor: Richard Warren]

Webster House Bed and Breakfast Inn - 1238 Versailles Avenue, Alameda; (510) 523-9697 [$75-$105]. Just minutes from Oakland, Webster House B & B is the oldest house in the city of Alameda. Friendly proprietors, Andrew and Susan

McCormack, have restored this 1854 Gothic Revival landmark where the amenities include an onsite Coffee and Tea House.

The Mansion at Lakewood - 1056 Hacienda Drive, in Walnut Creek; (510) 945-3600 [$135-$300]. A slightly more upscale accommodation than other Bay Area Bed & Breakfasts, the Mansion at Lakewood is an 1860 Victorian country manor. It's tucked away from the urban world on a serene three-acre estate containing magnolia, tecalpa, and persimmon heritage trees. Inside, rooms are cozy and guests are pampered. Beyond its white iron gates, are lovely boutique and antique shops in downtown Walnut Creek and, several miles south, the slopes of Mount Diablo. [Proprietors: Sharyn and Mike McCoy]

Restaurants

Bette's Oceanview Diner - 1807 4th Street in west Berkeley; (510) 644-3230. A popular west Berkeley breakfast and lunch spot, Bette's actually looks like a classic diner, and serves up fare that's just as memorable. No reservations.

Cafe de la Paz - 1600 Shattuck Avenue (upstairs) in north Berkeley; (510) 843-0662. Located in Berkeley's gourmet ghetto, this restaurant is a flavorful new comer with yummy tapas and innovative vegetarian and seafood entrees. This is Latin American cuisine with a refreshing California twist. Reservations recommended.

Cha-Am - 1543 Shattuck Avenue; (510) 848-9664. One of the more authentic Thai restaurants in the neighborhood, serving beef, chicken, and seafood entrees deliciously prepared with Thai herbs and curry sauces. Of special note is the red curry and *tom-ka gai*, a soup made with chicken carefully seasoned in a coconut milk broth. No reservations.

Chez Panisse Restaurant and Cafe - 1517 Shattuck Avenue; (510) 548-5525 (restaurant), 548-5049 (cafe). What else can we say about this world famous eatery that began dazzling diners in the early 1970s with wholesome foods? Featur-

ing fresh, locally grown ingredients, this wood frame establishment is chic yet homey. The downstairs restaurant offers a fixed
price menu. Reservations are required at the restaurant.

While everyone should experience dining in the restaurant
at least once (even Bill Clinton ate here), many prefer to eat in
the less formal, less expensive cafe upstairs. The food is just as
good and you order à la carte. No evening reservations are taken
at the cafe which can mean long waits on weekends.

Fat Apples - 1346 Martin Luther King Way; (510) 526-
2260. Jack London memorabilia decorates the walls in this
affordable eatery which serves an excellent breakfast, lunch, and
dinner. Hamburgers are the rage here, especially when topped
with a heaping mound of cheddar. Anything made with apples
is certain to please, but feel free to experiment. The olallie berry
pie is exceptional. The adjacent bakery also offers scrumptious
goodies to go. No reservations necessary.

Homemade Cafe - 2554 Sacramento Street; (510) 845-
1940. Open for breakfast and lunch, the Homemade Cafe is
considered by many to be Berkeley's best breakfast spot. This
quiet corner cafe offers hearty fare including fantastic homefries
in a relaxed and comfortable atmosphere. No reservations.

International House Cafe - 2299 Piedmont Avenue in
Berkeley; (510) 643-9932. Located at the top of Bancroft Way
beside Memorial Stadium, the I-House is frequently less crowded
than other cafes near the campus. This eatery offers a good
sandwich, soup, and salad selection in addition to standard cafe
pastries. Eavesdrop on foreign conversations while sipping coffee
and admiring an open view of the Golden Gate. No reservations.

La Mediterranee - 2936 College Avenue, near Ashby in
the Elmwood district; (510) 540-7773. A UC Berkeley graduate
student started this quality eatery, specializing in foods from
Armenia, Lebanon, and Greece. First timers should try the Meza,
a filling assortment of tasty Middle Eastern finger foods that
won't disappoint. No reservations.

Ristorante and Caffe Venezia - 1799 University Avenue in Berkeley; (510) 849-4681. Fresh and flavorful pasta dishes are the specialty here in this spacious Italian piazza-like setting, complete with a strung clothesline and central fountain. Moderately priced. Open daily for dinner and during the week for lunch. Reservations accepted.

Saul's Deli - 1475 Shattuck Avenue; (510) 848-3354. An authentic Jewish deli located in the Gourmet Ghetto, this is a good place to pick up some sandwiches to go.

Skates - 100 Seawall Drive at the foot of University Avenue in the Berkeley Marina; (510) 549-1900. Steak, seafood, and pasta dishes cooked every way imaginable is the fare in this slightly upscale bar and restaurant hosting one of the best Bayside views in the area. Reservations recommended.

Baywolf - 3853 Piedmont Avenue, Oakland; (510) 655-6004. California-style cuisine accented with French and Mediterranean touches make the menu here a winner. This unpretentious, wood-paneled eatery offers fine dining in a comfortable home-like atmosphere. Bay windows and a tasteful art collection grace this converted Victorian. On sunny days the elevated outdoor deck is the place to see and be seen.

Mama's Royal Cafe - 4012 Broadway, Oakland (510) 547-7600. A popular neighborhood eatery that's been in operation since 1973 and is well worth the expected wait on weekends. Serving up a scrumptious breakfast and lunch with generous portions, you can review annual Napkin Art Contest winners exhibited on the cafe walls. No reservations.

Market Hall - 5655 College Avenue in Rockridge. Food shops here include a bakery, produce market, wine shop, and gourmet market with cheese and pasta. You won't find sandwiches but the gourmet market offers a wide selection of unique and tasty salads which create a perfect picnic lunch; all you need to do is add a baguette, fruit, and specialty cheeses.

Oakland Grill - 301 Franklin, off Broadway in Oakland; (510) 835-1176. Tucked away in Oakland's historic produce market, this grill serves standard, quality fare for breakfast, lunch, and dinner at moderate prices. A good place to bring children, the converted warehouse is open and spacious. Reservations accepted.

Oliveto Cafe and Restaurant - 5655 College Avenue, part of the Market Hall complex in the Rockridge section of Oakland; (510) 547-5356. The inexpensive cafe/bar downstairs serves espresso drinks, beer and wine, specialty pizzas, and tasty tapas, while the moderately priced restaurant features rustic northern Italian entrees in a pleasant Mediterranean setting. Reservations necessary for the restaurant.

T.J.'s Gingerbread House - 741 5th Street; (510) 444-7373. Reservations are definitely required at this Oakland land-mark, featuring a scrumptious selection of Louisiana specialties including Whiskey stuffed lobster and sautéed quail. The Flamin-go pink architecture is a kick!

Tourelle Cafe & Restaurant - 3565 Mt. Diablo Boule-vard in Lafayette; (510) 284-3565. The large dining area is divided into several smaller, more intimate rooms, graced with wooden beams, brick walls, and copper trim. Diners feast on crostini, pizzettas, and excellent pasta dishes with generous por-tions. Quality eating at a moderate price. Live jazz is often fea-tured here, and the bar is a popular gathering spot. Reservations recommended.

East Bay Walks

Walk #1: Tilden Regional Park - Big Springs Trail

Walking Easy Time
2 hours

Named after Major Charles Lee Tilden, one of the instrumental figures establishing the East Bay Regional Park District, Tilden Regional Park, the first of the District's lands, has harbored many throughout history from the native Ohlone Tribes who hunted and gathered in these hills for centuries before the arrival of European explorers, to military troops stationed here during World War II. Only a short drive from Oakland and Berkeley downtowns, this park is an ideal getaway—with something to offer just about everyone—for locals and visitors alike, . Families with children will enjoy the swimming area at Lake Anza as well as the merry-go-round, steam trains, and pony rides. An 18-hole golf course rims the park for those who prefer a more civilized form of recreation, and, in addition to the designated nature area and botanical gardens, there are miles and miles of walking trails one shouldn't miss exploring.

Public transportation is available to this popular park on weekends and holidays. Catch the #67 bus near the Berkeley Bart station in downtown and get off at the Brazil Building. South Park Drive, where today's walk begins, is at the bottom of the grassy hillside extending from the building.

Directions: The easiest way to get to Tilden Regional Park by car is traveling north on Spruce Street from the UC Berkeley campus. Upon reaching the four-way intersection at the very top of the hill, continue straight across the road and descend along what is now Wildcat Canyon into the park. Either park in the lot near the Brazil Building or in the Camp Oaks parking area across from the Botanical Gardens where Wildcat Canyon and South Park Drive intersect.

Big Springs Trail makes for a gratifying, leisurely walk any-time of the day, but is particularly pleasant in the late afternoon, offering dazzling views of the sun setting over San Francisco and the Golden Gate. The first leg of the walk is the most chal-lenging but is also brief while the rest of the way entails a plea-sure-filled, relaxing traverse along the summit where fine eastern views extend all the way to Mount Diablo on clear days. Use the restroom at Camp Oaks parking area because there are no restrooms along the trail. There is only one picnic table situated on the trail which is not certain to be free, but walkers may eas-ily enjoy a pre- or post-walk picnic on the pleasant glade adja-cent to the Botanical Gardens.

Start: Locat-ed a half a mile up South Park Drive from the Botanical Gardens, this is where *Easy Walk-ers* find the trail head for today's walk. (During the winter and early spring months, South Park Drive is closed to protect migrating newts. If you happen to be visiting at this time, keep an eye out.) Take the right hand trail.

Big Springs Trail starts with a mild, gradual ascent winding towards the summit. A chaparral wilderness of scrub oak and coyote brush eventually gives way to soft grassy slopes, while glimpses of the Bay rise into view. Nearing the peak, Big Springs merges left with Sea View Trail which is also part of the East Bay Skyline National Trail, and the even larger Bay Area Ridge Trail that encircles the Bay.

San Francisco and the Golden Gate Bridge soon appear in full view on your left and, after traversing ahead, an open plateau welcomes similarly encompassing, eastern views of the San Pablo and Briones reservoirs shimmering below and majestic Mount Diablo beyond.

Your path, continuing along this crest for nearly a mile and a half, alternates sun-filled open vistas with cool, lush groves of Monterey pine. Just before descending, stop and rest at the lone picnic table and bench—a solitary outlook with additional views spanning nearly 270 degrees that capture Mount Tam, the eastern shores of Marin County, and, further in the distance, Napa and Sonoma counties. Almost equidistant with the Golden Gate's opening, there is quite a breeze flowing through here.

When you can tear yourself away, head north again along the same trail. The path eventually veers left 90 degrees and heads straight downwards into a stand of eucalyptus. Look for your reunion with Big Springs Trail—about five yards ahead and a hard left. The final leg proceeds along a narrower trail traversing the ridge at midsection. Views of San Francisco diminish with your descent while California poppies and star thistle cheerfully line the way come springtime. Halfway down you'll approach a fork. Take the high road which leads once again to South Park Drive, and where, after a right turn and another half mile, you're back at your car.

Walks #2 and #3: Briones Regional Park

In the shadow of Mount Diablo and tucked behind Tilden Regional Park, 5,000-acre Briones Regional Park is one of the East Bay's hidden treasures. There are no Bay views, only pleasant wilderness with each hill rolling endlessly into the next. Seasons are captured beautifully at Briones with the hills a rich green in the winter and early spring, turning to a soft gold in summer, and, come autumn, spectacular oranges and yellows.

Named after its original rancho owner, Felipe Briones, the park also maintains its ranching roots. For over 150 years Briones has been a grazing paradise, but today horses, mountain bikers, and walkers alike share in the park's idyllic pleasures.

Directions: Head east on State Highway 24 toward Walnut Creek. Several miles after the Caldecott Tunnel, make a left off the Orinda exit, and head northwest. Drive two miles and turn right on Bear Creek Road. Continue four and a half miles to Briones Road and the park entrance. Parking lots are available just beyond the park's kiosk. In the spring and summer months there is a small parking fee.

Walk #2: - Abrigo Valley Trail to Mott Peak Trail to Briones Crest Trail to Old Briones Road to Briones Road

Walking Easy Time
3 hours

Today's walk is quite steep in parts, making this four-mile loop through scenic canyons, meadows, and over graceful hilltops a challenging trek. Simply pace yourself and pause when necessary. Take a morning walk, before others arrive, and you may see deer, squirrels, and raccoons. There are no restrooms on the walk. Picnic facilities are available along Old Briones Road Trail and at park headquarters.

Start: Beginning at the Abrigo Valley Trail head, left of the kiosk on the northern side of the parking lot, you'll be using a fairly wide multipurpose trail, which means sharing the way with mountain bikers, horses, and cattle. Stay alert and follow the etiquette explained on pp. 28-29. You'll pass through several gates on this walk. Make sure to latch each one behind you, keeping the cattle on their respective ranges. The first leg of the walk, following alongside a shallow oak-filled cleft, is fairly level. A mile into the hike you'll approach another marker with a crossroad heading left. Proceed straight ahead, on the Mott Peak Trail.

The Mott Peak leg begins with a gradual ascent, becoming steeper as you climb. This half-mile stretch is the most difficult section you'll encounter. At the top of this trail you'll find soft, nearly open hillsides. Valley and coast live oak shade the terrain. Ahead of you is lofty Moss Peak. Continue on through another gate to the John Muir Nature Area. On your slow descent are great eastern views of Suisun Bay, Concord, Pleasant Hill, Walnut Creek, and Mount Diablo.

Turn right at the intersection of Moss Peak and Briones Crest trails and traverse the eastern slope of the mountain. Half a mile later the trail splits into three forks intersecting Old Briones Road. Here you'll make a right and carry on through the gate to complete your descent. Old Briones Road courses through one of Briones's scenic canyons with an elfin forest lining your path. The trail heads right, nearing the valley basin, remains level, and becomes paved after passing through the final gate. Briones Road leads back to the park kiosk and your car.

Walk #3: Deer Creek Trail to Pereira Trail

Walking Easy Time
3 hours

Here is another hike well worth the challenge. This four-mile out and back trek explores a less frequented area of the park characterized by stunning vistas and simple solitude. An especially beautiful sunset walk, past ponds and over ridges, the views of Briones Reservoir at the end of the road are postcard pretty.

Start: The trail head is located just off Briones Road, halfway between the park entrance and the kiosk. There is an unmarked post on the northern slope where walkers ascend to the left. Soon you'll reach the Deer Creek Trail marker. Proceed through the gate, following the left hand shore of the pond. This lightly tread section of the trail is a delight. You may even have to nego-tiate a harmless herd of cattle. Head northeast, paralleling Bear Creek Road until you reach a second pond and again, follow wide along the left hand side of this one. It's slightly marshy here so watch your footing and expect to get some mud on your shoes. There is no specific trail marker on the other side of the pond, but you'll be able to see the vague outline of a path lead-ing slightly right and uphill. This is Pereira Trail, the quickest way to reach some of the park's finest peaks where you'll enjoy views of adjacent summits and broad valleys. Reaching the end of the path, rest on the lone bench at the look out area and enjoy picturesque Briones Reservoir. Just minutes from the city, this semi-wilderness is a great escape for the *Easy Walker*.

Walk #4: Mount Diablo State Park - Juniper, Pioneer and Summit Loop

Walking Easy Time
3½ hours

Mount Diablo hovers above the city of Danville in Contra Costa County. At 3,849 feet, the highest summit in the Bay Area, it is famous for its panoramic views which extend on clear days for nearly 200 miles. Like most of the East Bay and espe-cially the Coastal Range, Diablo is characterized by oak wood-lands, dry grassland, and a chaparral covered landscape. With over 100 miles of trails and diverse vegetation, this is a walker's paradise. The best time to visit Mount Diablo is the early spring. After winter rains the hills, a stunning green, are emblematic of an Irish landscape. We suggest you make this a morning hike. Because this walk is near the summit, there is not much shade, and the heat is often extreme in the summer months.

Directions: Unfortunately there is no access to the park via public transportation. Mount Diablo is easily accessible, however, by car. Located off Interstate 680 in Danville, take the Diablo Road exit going east. Remain on Diablo Road and signs will direct you to the park.

Once you're in the park, continue your driving ascent and you'll eventually arrive at the junction of North Gate, South Gate and Summit roads. Head east, up Summit Road until you arrive at Juniper Campground (on your left). Park in the overlook area. The trailhead is located near the Laurel Dell Group Picnic Area just behind the recycling bins, right of the campground entrance.

The Juniper - Pioneer - Summit Loop is a comfortable walk with an ascent of 1,200 feet. Broken down into three stages, each leg encounters different life zones within the park. As you climb the views of the valley and larger Bay Area become more spectacular and panoramic. (After the Juniper leg of this walk we strongly suggest taking a slight detour. The short **Fire Interpretive Trail** at the summit is an easy traverse adding another half hour to the walk, and offers incomparable panoramic views of the Bay Area and beyond.)

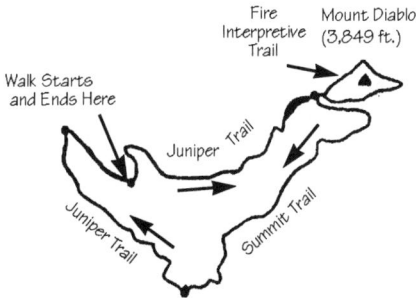

Start: The first leg (Juniper - Pioneer) of this walk climbs toward the summit. Narrow switchbacks turn into straight ascents, making this the most strenuous part of the walk. The trail, however, is easy to follow. Try exploring some of the forks leading to clearings with stunning scenery of the broad valley below. As you climb note that the woodland vegetation thins out and views become more expansive. Stay on the main chaparral-lined path, heading toward the anomalous communications tower and your path will eventually intersect Summit Road.

Cross to the other side of the road where a marker guides walkers up towards another communications tower and beyond that, an unexpected parking lot. Head across this paved expanse to the lower parking lot where you'll find bathrooms as well as an interpretive center. The second leg of the trail continues at the southern end of this lot.

If you're feeling energetic and crave fabulous views, add an extra 20 to 30 minutes to your walk by exploring the **Fire Interpretive Trail**. It's an easy walk, not far from where you are. Continue up Summit Road after exiting the lower lot and veer left; you won't miss the trailhead. This level trek circles the mountain near its peak. Lofty Mount Diablo is surrounded for miles by mere foothills which accounts for such expansive views unparalleled by none, except maybe 19,000-foot Mount Kilimanjaro. At certain vantage points (North and East) there are charts which illustrate and name the various peaks, canyons, and other landmarks you see in the distance. Complete the circle and arrive once again on Summit Road. Continue left down the road and return to the parking lot. The trail head for the second leg (Pioneer - Summit) of today's loop is on your left.

Begin your descent here. The trail is substantially wider as you forge through open country and delve into a thicket of scrub oak and manzanita. Southern views of soft rolling hills on your left are never-ending and complemented in springtime by the subtle, pleasant scent of buckbrush in bloom.

As you continue down you'll reach the Pioneer Horse Camp. If no one is around this is a nice place to stop and have lunch. There are some picnic tables next to the bathtub-cum-makeshift watering trough. If you prefer to wait for some shade and the end of the walk before eating, simply continue down the path as you're nearing the third and final leg.

Your path leads out onto a paved road where you'll make a right. Before this road intersects Summit Road pause and note the distant view of hills framed by the scenic canyon crevice to the left.

Cross Summit Road via the cross walk and continue 35 yards down the dirt road. You'll find the third trailhead on your right. This section is our favorite part of the walk. In the spring, grassy hillsides along Moses Rock Ridge are green and dotted with orange poppies and purplish lupine.

The path begins with a short switchback climb, crosses a

dirt road, and continues on more level terrain. In spring, you'll enjoy the park's verdant splendor as smooth grassy hills alternate with the darker shades of an elfin forest, while the view opens to encompass the picturesque valley below. The trail will reach a spacious clearing where you come across another watering trough. The campground is just beyond, and slightly to your right. Continue up through the campground and you will arrive once again at the lookout point and your car.

Walk #5: Redwood Regional Park - Stream Trail to Fern Trail to French Trail and return on West Ridge

Walking Easy Time
3½ hours

Straddling both Contra Costa and Alameda counties, Redwood Regional Park is a unique section of the East Bay Regional Park District. Here the region's characteristic oak woodlands and spacious rolling grasslands give way to a handsome remnant of the 300-foot high coast redwoods that once spanned a five-square-mile region. Greedy settlers who found the lumber business more lucrative than mining devastated this area which provided the foundation for San Francisco's burgeoning growth.

Today a second generation of redwoods is seen, protected by the East Bay Regional Park District. Redwood Regional Park offers a pleasant, shady alternative during the warm summer months. It's the perfect recreational enclave for jogging, mountain biking, horseback riding, and, of course, *Easy Walking*.

Directions: The easiest way to get to Redwood Regional Park is to take the Joaquin Miller exit off State Highway 13. Head east up the hill, and turn left onto Skyline Boulevard. Follow Skyline north for another five miles and park at the Skyline Gate Staging Area.

A canyon descent along Stream Trail eases walkers into the heart of this young redwood stand. The return along evergreen shaded French Trail, a mid-ridge traverse, presents more of a challenge to the *Easy Walker*. Cool and shady most of the way, we recommend lunching at Mill Site or Fern Hut, located midway on today's five-mile walk. Other picnic facilities and restrooms dot Stream Trail.

Start: The Stream trailhead is located just beyond the water fountain at the Skyline Gate Staging area. Today's walk descends half a mile from the side crest, past scrub oak, coyote brush, and scatterings of orange sticky monkey flower, down into the canyon before heading through redwood territory.

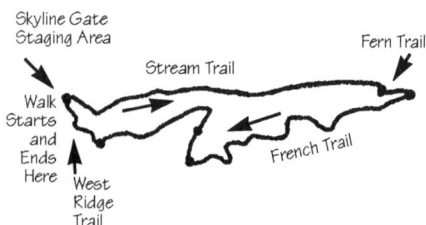

Passing first through Girl's Camp (one of several picnic facilities along this trail) the chaparral-lined pathway is warm and dry, then begins to cool off as you enter the shade of the redwood forest. Redwood Creek parallels the trail, contributing to the lush setting. Look for redwood rings, bands of redwoods forming a circle around a hollow space where a parent tree once stood. These tell the story of this region's logging heritage.

Remain on Stream Trail for one and a half miles, passing Mill Site and Fern Hut—pleasant picnic rest areas where you may want to pause before beginning the return trek along French Trail.

At the far end of Fern Hut, turn right at the first marker and left at the next. Fern Trail, bridging Stream and French trails, is short, but steep, and one of this walk's most challenging sections.

Turn right at the intersection of Fern and French trails (there is no clear marker here). Narrower than Stream Trail, French Trail leads through the redwood thicket blanketed with sorrel and braken fern. In the damp winter months look for unique mushroom species thriving in this moist forest environment.

Just over a mile into this trail you'll cross two stream beds. After the second, French Trail briefly merges right with Tres

Sendas Trail. One hundred yards further on, French Trail breaks left and climbs through stands of madrones and scrub oak (look for Douglas irises in springtime) before reaching the well-trafficked West Ridge Trail. Making a right here, this trail (beware of mountain bikers) leads you back to the parking area.

Walk #6: Lake Chabot Regional Park - East Shore Trail to Honker Bay Trail to Columbine Trail to Bass Cove Trail and return on West Shore Trail

Walking Easy Time
5 hours

Lake Chabot is the product of the late 1800s when water companies were scooping up East Bay lands and damming them for water and profit. Unlike other East Bay watershed regions, deemed surplus and sold off, this lake is still owned by the East Bay Municipal Utility District. Named for the engineer who created it, Anthony Chabot, it is now leased to the East Bay Regional Park District and open to the public for recreational purposes. Today, Lake Chabot Regional Park is perfect for the family outing or lone getaway. Always well stocked with bass and trout, this is one of the most popular fishing spots in the East Bay. Most of the activity centers around the Marina where boat rentals, picnic facilities, cafe, and playing fields are located. Crowds are easily left behind by venturing beyond the marina to explore the lake's quieter shores.

Directions: Heading east on Interstate 580 take the Fairmont Drive exit. Continue east toward the hills where Fairmont turns into Lake Chabot Road. Signs for the Lake Chabot Marina are posted on the left. Parking is available inside the park for a small fee or on Lake Chabot Road.

All five of these trails intersect to form one large loop tracing placid Lake Chabot. Each leg offers a different vantage point for views of the lake and illustrates another life zone, giving the *Easy Walker* a feel for the this park's diversity.

Picnic and rest areas dot East and West Shore trails which are the first and final legs of today's walk. Bathrooms are plentiful but water is not, so make sure you bring along plenty of water for the journey.

Bass Cove Trail
Columbine Trail
Honker Bay Trail
West Ridge Trail
East Ridge Trail
Walk Starts and Ends Here
Marina

Start: At the entrance, follow the main path leading toward the Marina. At the fork turn right, and pass through the Turtle picnic area, merging onto East Shore Trail— the beginning of today's lengthy excursion. After passing through Tadpole Meadow, Willard, and Mallard group picnic areas, continue straight ahead on the level path, shared with bikers and joggers. Recreational fishermen dot the shore here and out on Live Oak Island.

As you continue east through the cream bush and cow parsnip, the crowds thin out. Various coves and landings descend off the main path if you want to relax for a spell near the shore shaded by oaks. There are also several scenic and cozy picnic spots above the trail if you decide to fuel up for the walk.

A mile and a half later, the East Shore Trail pavement ends. Follow the dirt path to a footbridge and Honker Bay Trail, the second leg of today's walk. After crossing the bridge, continue another 20 yards and head left at the next junction. The feel of the Honker Bay Trail is much different; the East Shore Trail's cool shade gives way to warmer temperatures and dry chaparral.

A mile down the trail your route ascends inland. As you climb, oak and pine give way to fragrant eucalyptus towering above. Lake views from this vantage point are excellent.

On your way up you'll reach a sign reading "Lake Chabot Bicycle Loop." Just beyond this point the switchbacked

Columbine Trail leads left and down through eucalyptus and red-woods. This wooded two-and-a-half-mile route eventually merges with Bass Cove Trail. Remain alert for mountain bikers here as the trail widens and heads left near the shoreline.

Bass Cove Trail dead ends at the paved intersection where West Shore Trail begins. Continue left, across Chabot Dam to reach this path, studded with oak foliage similar to the East Shore Trail. As you near the Marina along West Shore's one-and-a-half mile stretch, you'll rejoin the park's other visitors and ease your way back into civilization.

Walk #7: Sunol Regional Wilderness - Indian Joe Creek Trail to Cave Rocks Road to Cerro Este Road and back on Canyon View Trail

Walking Easy Time
3 hours

A step back in time, Sunol Regional Wilderness has changed little from its Spanish past. Verdant hills, narrow canyons, streams, and in spring, small waterfalls make this pastureland a delight. Along the trail, samples of sandstone, greenstone, schist, and metachert tell of a time when this area was submerged beneath the sea. More recently, bedrock mortars used by Ohlone Indians to crush acorns from giant oaks have been discovered here. Remnants of Sunol's past are displayed in the tiny, yet comprehensive, visitor center located near the park's headquarters. There you can also pick up a pamphlet, detailing Sunol's pioneer history. Three ranches purchased by Willis Brinker in the 1930s were later given to the park district when he passed away becoming Sunol Regional Park in 1959. Exploring this 5,974-acre wilderness, from the lush depths of Alameda Creek, to the dry, exposed Diablo heights, you'll find Sunol in the 90s offers a clear view of this handsome region's past.

Directions: Take the Calaveras Road exit, off Interstate

680 just outside of the town of Sunol. Drive several miles south, following signs for the park's central headquarters, and turn left on Geary road which leads to the park's main entrance.

There is something very serene about Sunol, especially in the early morning or late afternoon. The leisurely climb through lush Indian Canyon leads out onto spacious fields, and up along rolling hills to memorable viewpoints. As one of the lesser known East Bay parks, patrons are few and the solitude, sublime.

Start: Today's easy walk begins along the narrow paved footpath extending right from the park's visitor center. Bear left when you hit the bridge crossing Alameda Creek. Veer right off the bridge and head toward Indian Joe Creek Trail via the level, quarter-mile stretch along Canyon View Trail.

Indian Rocks

Cave Roaks Road

Indian Joe Creek Trail

Walk Starts and Ends Here

Este Road

Cerro

Canyon View Trail

After a brief ascent, Indian Joe Creek Trail splits left and you'll enter grazing lands. This initial stretch takes you up the slightly graded Indian Canyon. Indian Joe, claiming to be a native, worked for the Geary family who originally squatted here. He lived in a milkshed near the creek that runs through this canyon until his death in 1950.

Coloring the creek's bank and lining your path, orange sticky monkey flower nestles among the willow and sycamore trees. Ascending further, you'll find stands of California laurels and you may catch sight of a steller's jay or brown towhee amidst the manzanita or coast live oak.

A mile along this trail, you'll reach the Indian rock caves. A rare mixture of basalt (greenstone) and schist, this stone conglomeration, popular with rock climbers, is also a good spot for a makeshift picnic.

On the road again, the trail continues another quarter mile before nearing the top and intersecting with Cave Rocks Road.

Here you'll turn right, traverse the open ridge, and enjoy splendid views of the opposite crest where light brown, softly sculptured hills are speckled with chaparral patches and verdant valley oak.

Cave Rocks Road climbs slightly before heading down toward the Cerro Este Overlook and Road. Turn right on Cerro Este Road and pause for a southwesterly view of the Calaveras Reservoir before beginning your final descent.

Follow the markers down a steep grade towards "Little Yosemite." Traces of sandstone appear in the barren grassy hillsides.

Curving left, you'll approach a junction marked by a barbed wire fence and watering trough. Beyond the fence is the Ohlone Wilderness where access requires a special permit. Canyon View Trail, the final leg of today's walk, leads right.

Veer left at a vague fork 50 yards into this trail. From this point your route traverses another ridge sloping steeply toward Alameda Creek, offering views of the scenic, miniature valley, "Little Yosemite," below.

Blue oak and buckeye trees shade your route down to this stream that is a special delight in the springtime. Follow its eastern bank, cross the bridge, and return to reality.

Walk #8: Coyote Hills Regional Park - Bayview Trail to Nike Trail to Bayview Trail to Pelican Trail to Alameda Creek Trail to D.U.S.T. Trail and return along the Boardwalk

Walking Easy Time
3 hours

Once embracing over two-million acres, America's wetlands have dwindled by 50 percent, lost to farming and industrial interests which have filled in this precious resource from sea to shining sea. On the east shore of the San Francisco Bay, miles and miles of wetlands have been lost to 20th century development. Most of that land, off the shores of Oakland and Berkeley, has been filled. Fortunately one of the few remaining protected wetland areas in the United States, is found at Coyote Hills Regional Park. The diverse wetlands at Coyote Hills include fresh water marshes, salt evaporation ponds, grass lands, and small hillsides. They harbor over 200 species of birds and other wildlife.

Over 2,400 years ago the Ohlone Indians, who inhabited most of the East Bay Region, occupied this land. Remnants of their presence is found in four shellmounds located within the park. After Spanish, Mexican, and white settlers decimated the thriving Indian communities, this land served hunting, industrial, and military needs. Finally, in 1968, it was set aside as a wildlife sanctuary.

In addition to offering a variety of intriguing walking environments, Coyote Hills is one of the East Bay's less frequented parks, a place where the past is very much alive.

Directions: From Interstate 880 in the East Bay, exit onto State Highway 84, heading toward the Dumbarton Bridge. Take the Paseo Padre Parkway North, before reaching the Bridge, and turn left on Patterson Ranch Road which leads into the park. (Visitors with vehicles are charged a small parking fee.)

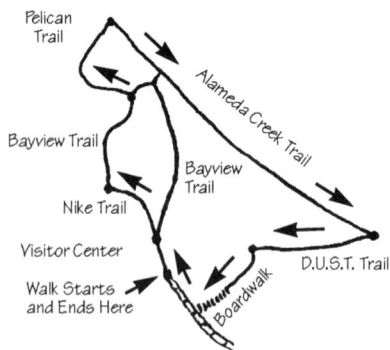

We've linked sections of several different trails together within this 1,064-acre refuge to provide a sample of the various habitats. The elevation varies little on this easy walk and there are several opportunities to return to the visitor center, making today's walk as short or long as you like. Restrooms are located only near the visitor center. Picnic facilities are also found near the visitor center and scattered along Alameda Creek Trail.

Start: From the visitor center head north along the paved road you took into the park. This section of the Bayview trail leads toward Alameda Creek. After 100 yards, veer left onto the dirt fire road, Nike Trail, which leads across the grassy hillside. This vantage point is a great place to photograph the verdant fresh water marshes behind you.

The spacious Nike Trail crosses paths with Red Hill Trail and then descends towards the colorful Salt Evaporation Ponds on the other side of the hill. In the distance are the San Mateo and Dumbarton Bridges. When the Nike and Bayview trails intersect you'll turn right and parallel the salty shoreline. Keep an eye out for a double-crested cormorant or Western sandpiper.

At the wooden view platform, descend the steps and proceed on the Pelican Trail toward the Bay. This mile-long dirt mound cuts through the salt ponds, providing close access to this unusual seaside refuge. (You may bypass the Pelican Trail by continuing north on the Bay View Trail until it meets with Alameda Creek Trail via a short spur trail.)

Pelican Trail exits onto the gravelly Alameda Creek Trail, a long, straight, and narrow stretch paralleling the Creek. This popular route, shared with bikers and joggers, splits the creek on your left from the marshes on your right and extends inland. (If you've taken Pelican Trail and now prefer to head back to the visitor center, bypassing Alameda Creek Trail, take the spur trail toward Bayview Trail where the gravel path becomes paved.)

Slightly elevated, Alameda Creek Trail lends a nice overview of the expansive fresh water marshes on your right. Several picnic benches offer a respite in shady groves along this trail.

Backtracking right, off the Alameda Creek Trail, D.U.S.T. Trail is the final leg of today's walk. After a dirt path diagonally crosses D.U.S.T. Trail, look left and you can see one of the four remaining Indian shellmounds in Coyote Hills Regional Park. These mounds, containing discarded relics such as shellfish, human skeletons and other artifacts, document the campsites of Coyote Hills's original inhabitants.

Instead of completing D.U.S.T. Trail, take the first path heading left, and explore the marsh's fascinating maze. As you follow signs directing your return to the visitor center, the trail veers slightly right, onto a long wooden footbridge or boardwalk. Out beyond the cattails and sedges are open patches of water where you can look for common ruddy ducks or the rare tunda swan.

SOUTH BAY

South of San Francisco is another of those peculiar anomalies that makes northern California such a special place for *Easy Walkers*. Within minutes of the city's boundaries are vast parks, watersheds, and coastal retreats that can instantly take you back in time. As you move further down the peninsula you will be able to enjoy a network of county, regional, and state parks, as well as redwood forests ranging from the mountains to the seashore. Plan your route correctly and you spend days without seeing a freeway, a shopping center or even a stop sign.

Most of these retreats are within an hour of cities like Palo Alto, San Jose, and Santa Cruz. You can hike for days, if you wish, coming out of the wilderness to enjoy the creature comforts of college towns, the Silicon Valley and, of course, San Francisco itself. Or if you prefer, choose one of the exciting urban parks. From rock outcroppings, oak woodlands, to virgin growth forests, the South Bay, including San Mateo, Santa Clara, and Santa Cruz counties, offers trails perfect for hikes of any length.

One of the intriguing features of this region is its rich and fascinating history. The Ohlone Indians lived here along the region's bay and coastal shores. Convinced that their world had been created by the hummingbird, eagle, and coyote, they were easy prey for the Spanish missionaries who built their first mission at Santa Clara in 1777.

Efforts to civilize the Indians led to their untimely demise; the white man's diseases diminished their numbers. The first inhabitants lost their lands to these missionaries and later to the Mexican government. Their lands were divided into ranchos that were later sold to white settlers who had come for the Gold Rush and stayed to make their fortunes through ranching, logging, and mercantilism.

Fortunately, many of these earlier settlers realized, unlike their brethren on the East Bay, that wilderness had its purpose. Instead of slashing all the forests, farsighted pioneers began a campaign to save the best of the redwood forests in Santa Cruz County. New watersheds protected to quench the thirst of the cities to the north, became another recreational asset. And tourism became a viable business as city slickers headed south via rail to enjoy the many pleasures of the South Bay, particularly the Santa Cruz mountains.

One of the forces moving this region in the right direction was a strong tradition of higher education. Leland Stanford, who made his fortune in the Gold Rush, left much of it to the University that bears his name. An architectural landmark well worth a visit, the University's sandstone museum features such highlights as the golden spike sunk by Stanford at the junction of the Union Pacific and Central Pacific railroads in Promontory Point, Utah.

Besides being one of the nation's leading institutions of higher learning, Stanford is also one of the prettiest campuses in America. The historic Quad, fountains at every turn, a small lake, plazas, and parks make Stanford's "Farm" a great place to explore. At the east end of the campus, University Avenue leads into a lively downtown district filled with fine shops, great restaurants, and bookstores—a place that's perfect for a night on the town.

When the history of the 20th century is written there will no doubt be a section on another of the South Bay's major achievements, Silicon Valley. Stretching roughly south from the Palo Alto area to San Jose, this region is the birthplace of the semiconductor, the microchip, and the personal computer. The region's dominant industry, this high tech citadel has become a world capital of technology. Once known for its prunes (in the 1960s nearly a third of California's fruit was grown in Santa Clara County), this region is now a kind of high tech swapmeet where initial public offerings turn nerds into moguls overnight.

In this high stakes land where computation speed is everything, it's not surprising that people feel a need to slow down and get back to the land whenever they can. Understandably the communities of the South Bay, now more than ever, value their backyard wilderness.

Today this region offers hundreds of hiking opportunities, from Coyote Point south of San Francisco Airport to Mount Hamilton southeast of San Jose. Many of the best parks have been created over the past thirty years. Old quicksilver mines like New Almaden have been turned into county parks. Bay Frontage in Mountain View and Palo Alto has become superb birdwatching territory. Taking their lead from the East Bay Regional Park District, residents here created the Midpeninsula Regional Open Space District in 1972. Similar efforts at the city, county, and state level have expanded parklands and historic districts throughout the region.

For those craving steeper territory, the mountain parks of San Mateo and Santa Cruz counties are easily accessed by State Highways 35 and 9.

A popular weekend hub, Santa Cruz, is one of northern California's most distinguished beach towns. Home of a beautiful University of California campus, this town has bounced back nicely from the devastating 1989 Loma Prieta earthquake. Beautiful Victorians, the state's oldest roller coaster, a surfing museum, and miles of peaceful beaches make this community a great base for *Easy Walkers*.

The region's largest town, one easily overlooked by wilderness enthusiasts, is San Jose. While it may lack the amenities of San Francisco, this community is blessed with a number of intriguing attractions such as the one-of-a-kind Winchester Mystery House, a high technology museum and a first class children's museum.

Wherever you go in the South Bay, you're likely to find yourself tempted to stay longer. Because this region's attractions aren't as well known as San Francisco's, you're likely to find more privacy along the streams and rivers, forest paths, and secluded ocean coves. Come when you can. Stay as long as possible. The rewards are many and you'll certainly want to return again and again.

The Feel of Walks in the South Bay

From the vast and varied wilderness of bountiful oaks rimming the Santa Clara Valley to the majestic redwoods of the

Santa Cruz Mountains, the region south of San Francisco offers *Easy Walkers* a wide choice of scenic trails and diverse terrain.

How to get to the Counties South of San Francisco

Interstate 280 and Highway 101 are the main thorough-fares linking San Francisco with its southern neighbors. State Highway 35 is the scenic route through San Mateo County, also leading to many of its spectacular parks.

Highway 101 passes through San Jose (along with inter-states 880 and 680 if you're coming from the East Bay) while Interstate 280 takes you downtown.

State Highway 17 from San Jose is the main route to Santa Cruz, but you can also get there via scenic Highways 9 through the mountains or 1 along the coast.

Sights and Excursions in the South Bay

San Jose in Santa Clara County, the main urban hub south of San Francisco, is where you'll find many of the sights listed below. While San Mateo and Santa Cruz counties attract visi-tors with rich forests and natural scenery, there are also worth-while manmade attractions scattered across the mountains and along the coast.

1. Stanford University Art Gallery. (Open 10 to 5 Tues-day through Friday; 1 to 5 Saturday and Sunday; (415) 723-2842.) A great University museum, the Stanford Art Gallery showcases intriguing exhibits including "Travel Around the World," a collection of prints, drawings, and photographs on travel throughout history by artists from Piranesi to Turner. The museum also features art from different cultures such as "The Arts of Buddhism" from the beginnings of Buddhism through the 19th century, and religious art from Renaissance and Baroque Europe.

Directions: Located on Serra Street near Hoover Tower on the Stanford University Campus in Palo Alto.

2. Filoli. (Open February through September; (415) 346-2880.) A 654-acre estate, Filoli is a spectacular country-house-style mansion with forty-three rooms. It was the original set for television's "Dynasty."

Directions: Located on Canada Road. South of Highway 92 in Woodside.

3. Winchester Mystery House. (Open 9 to 8 daily; (408) 247-2101.) Twenty-four hours a day for thirty-eight years, Sarah Winchester continued to build this bizarre Victorian Mansion. Rifle heiress and eccentric, Winchester thought she could extend her life as long as the house remained under construction. The California Historic Landmark has four stories and 160 rooms with staircases leading nowhere and doors opening into walls designed to confuse the spirits of firearm victims.

Directions: 525 South Winchester Boulevard between Stevens Creek Boulevard and Interstate 280 in San Jose.

4. San Jose Museum of Art. (Open 10 to 5 Tuesday through Sunday; 10 to 8 on Thursdays; (408) 294-2787.) Robert Arneson, David Best, Rupert Garcia, and Robert Hudson are just a few of the contemporary artists featured at the San Jose Museum of Art which boasts a comprehensive selection of 20th-century artwork. This museum is currently in the midst of its most memorable exhibition; for 3 years it's displaying over 100 American pieces (featured in two exhibitions) from New York's Whitney Museum of American Art.

Directions: 110 South Market Street at San Fernando.

5. The Tech Museum of Innovation. (Open 10 to 5 Tuesday through Sunday; (408) 279-7150.) This interactive, high-tech, and hands-on museum keeps visitors up to date on the Silicon Valley's achievements and showcases emerging technology. Gallery exhibits range from bicycles to computers to robotics. The weekly speaker series is always enlightening.

Directions: 145 West San Carlos Street, across from the Convention Center.

6. Children's Discovery Museum of San Jose. (Open 10 to 5 Tuesday through Saturday; 12 to 5 Sunday; (408) 298-

5437.) One of the nation's largest children's museums, this one teaches kids from two to 13 about the latest in technology, science, and the arts. The galleries offer many interactive and special exhibits.

Directions: 180 Woz Way, near Auzerais and W. San Carlos Street.

7. San Jose Historical Museum. (Open 10 to 4:30 Monday through Friday, 12 to 4:30 Saturday and Sunday; (408) 287-2290.) This living history park encompasses 25 acres that depict downtown San Jose's evolution from the 1880s to the present day. Along the way you'll see 25 lifesize structures including interior exhibits from the old Pacific Hotel, a traditional soda fountain, a firehouse, and even a 1927 gasoline station.

Also on permanent display is San Jose's *Ng Shing Gung*, an 1880 Chinese Temple.

Directions: 635 Phelan Avenue, in San Jose's Kelley Park.

8. Kelley Park. A 150-acre urban park with picnic and recreation facilities, Kelley Park includes a children's petting zoo, Japanese friendship garden, and puppet shows. It's also home to the San Jose Historical Museum.

Directions: Bounded by Keyes and Senter Road.

9. Villa Montalvo. (Open 9 to 5 daily; (408) 741-3421.) This magnificent 19-room Mediterranean-style mansion was the home of James Phelan, three-term mayor of San Francisco and a popular US Senator. Today it's a cultural center featuring exhibits, events, and summer concerts held on the spacious grounds where you can also roam graceful gardens and a woodsy arboretum.

Directions: 15400 Montalvo Road, in Saratoga.

10. Lick Observatory. (Open 12:45 to 5 daily; (408) 274-5061.) A gift to the people of California from James Lick, this Observatory is the astronomy and astrophysics research station for the University of California. Here you can see a 36-inch refracting and 120-inch reflecting telescope in addition to other instruments that delight science buffs.

Directions: Follow Highway 130, 25 miles southeast of San Jose, to the top of Mount Hamilton.

☞ **HINT: With all of the excitement over Napa and Sonoma county wines, many overlook the Bay Area's southern wine region which is just as respectable. Drop in for a tour and taste at Mirassou Vineyards (3000 Aborn Road; (408) 274-4000) in San Jose, or Byington Winery (21850 Bear Creek Road; (408) 354-1111) in Los Gatos. Ask your hotel proprietor for other suggestions.**

11. Roaring Camp and Big Trees Narrow-Gauge Railroad. (408) 335-4484. Through giant redwood forests, along steep cliffs, across the San Lorenzo River, and countless valleys and canyons, Roaring Camp and Big Trees Railroad takes you from the Santa Cruz Beach Boardwalk to the top of Bear Mountain. Originally used to transport gold diggers and lumbermen into the mountains, today it's one of the last steam-powered passenger railroads.

Ask about Saturday evening moonlight rides which also include dinner and entertainment. Open daily, call for current schedule.

Directions: The depot is located a half a mile from the town of Felton on Graham Hill and Mount Hermon roads at Roaring Camp in Santa Cruz County.

12. Santa Cruz Beach and Boardwalk. (408) 426-7433. California's last beach-side amusement park, with 20 rides, some dating back to the 1911 Loolf carousel and 1924 Giant Dipper rollercoaster. Set astride a mile-long beach, special events are hosted year round on the Boardwalk such as the "Summertime, Summer Nights," a series of free Friday evening concerts featuring live bands.

Directions: The Boardwalk is located at 400 Beach Street at the north end of Monterey Bay via State highways 1 or 17.

Accommodations

Old Thyme Inn Bed & Breakfast - 779 Main Street in San Mateo's Half Moon Bay; (415) 726-1616 [$75-220]. A quaint Queen Anne Victorian dating back to 1899, this cozy seaside Bed and Breakfast is beautifully furnished with period antiques. Each of the seven guest rooms, named after herbs growing in the garden, is warmly decorated with stuffed animals. A full breakfast is served in the central parlor. Afterwards guests can stroll along the ocean or make their way to one of San Mateo's many beautiful parks. [Innkeepers: George and Marcia Dempsey]

Cowper Inn - 705 Cowper Street, at Forest Street in Palo Alto; (415) 327-4475, fax (415) 329-1703 [$55-105]. Nestled in a quiet residential neighborhood not far from downtown Palo Alto, Stanford University, and the popular Stanford Shopping Center, is the cozy Cowper Inn. Guests stay in oddly shaped, yet comfortable rooms. They also enjoy the parlor and sitting rooms gracing this lovely Victorian. Join other guests for afternoon wine served outdoors on the porch when the weather is pleasant. [Proprietor: Peggy Woodworth]

The Victorian on Lytton - 555 Lytton Avenue in Palo Alto; (415) 322-8555, fax (415) 322-7141 [$98-200]. Boasting ten rooms with private baths, down comforters, and four poster or canopy beds, this lovely Victorian was built in 1895 and fully restored in 1986. Guests enjoy a continental breakfast served in their rooms, complimentary evening sherry, and a splendid English Garden. [Innkeepers: Maxwell and Susan Hall]

The Hensley House - 456 N. Third Street, San Jose; (408) 298-3537, fax (408) 298-4676 [$75-155]. Enjoy high tea Thursdays and Saturdays and wine and hors d'oeuvres every other afternoon at this elegantly decorated San Jose guest house. Four of the five rooms are named after San Jose historical figures. Each is made warm and comfortable with period antiques plus modern amenities such as phones, televisions, and VCRs. Just minutes from downtown, guests also have access to the nearby private athletic club in case you want an extra workout for the day. [Innkeepers: Sharon Layne and Bill Priest]

The Babbling Brook Inn - 1025 Laurel Street, Santa Cruz; (408) 427-2437, fax (408) 427-2457 [$85-150]. As the name suggests, a refreshing stream complete with a cascading waterfall decorates the lush rustic garden of this lovely Bed and Breakfast Inn built in 1909 on the foundations of a 1790s grist mill and 1870s tannery. Each room is uniquely decorated with stained glass windows, hardwood floors, and French doors. Many have views of the garden and some come with their own private deck. In addition to a hearty country breakfast and complimentary wine and cheese each afternoon, don't forget to help yourself to some of Helen's homemade cookies. [Innkeeper: Helen King]

Chateau Victorian - 118 First Street, Santa Cruz; (408) 458-9458 [$110-140]. Originally built as a single family home at the turn of the century and converted into apartments in the 1950s, this cozy Bed and Breakfast Inn was completely renovated in the early 1980s. Today, guests enjoy comfortable rooms, each with a warm personal fireplace, and a continental breakfast served in the lounge. Ideally located, Chateau Victorian is just a block away from the ocean shore, the wharf, and popular Santa Cruz Boardwalk. [Innkeeper: Alice June]

Cliff Crest Bed & Breakfast Inn - 407 Cliff Street, Santa Cruz; (408) 427-2609 [$85-135]. Snugly situated near the ocean, this Queen Anne Victorian offers five private and beautifully furnished rooms in a hospitable setting. Guests are encouraged to lounge by the cozy sitting-room fireplace or explore the grounds designed by John McLaren, who shaped Golden Gate Park. [Innkeepers: Sharon & Bruce Taylor]

The Inn at Depot Hill - 250 Monterey Avenue, Capitola-by-the-Sea, just south of Santa Cruz; (408) 462-3376, fax (408) 462-3697 [$165-250]. A converted turn-of-the-century railroad depot, this is an upscale inn for the traveler who enjoys creature comforts and all of the amenities. Four large rooms and four additional suites, one with private entrance and personal garden, have been meticulously decorated to create a romantic destination; hence the Delft Room, Stratford-on-Avon, Cote d'Azur, and others. The rest of the inn is just as impressive with ceilings rising sixteen feet and a parlor featuring an antique piano. Gardens surround a pleasant herringboned brick patio overlooking beautiful Monterey Bay. The *trompe l'oeil* dining room makes you feel as if you're eating breakfast in a train's dining car. [Innkeeper: Suzanne Lankes]

Restaurants

The Dining Room - 1602 S. El Camino Real, San Mateo; (415) 493-4542. Located in a charming cottage, this handsome restaurant features continental dining. Beautiful antiques add to the charm.

JoAnn's B Street Cafe - 30 B Street at First, San Mateo; (415) 347-7000. Omelets, French toast, waffles, and pastries are all popular at this traditional diner. The portions are huge and the prices are fair. Good homestyle cooking.

San Benito House - Mill and Main Streets, Half Moon Bay; (415) 726-3425. This circa 1905 establishment is the place to enjoy pizza, ravioli, squash soup, and fresh seafood. Drawing heavily on locally grown ingredients, the charming San Benito House is also well known for its chocolate cake. Yum.

Cafe Pro Bono - 2437 Birch Street, Palo Alto; (415) 326-1626. This cafe is known for dishes such as char-broiled marinated jumbo prawns with roasted red pepper puree and feta cheese, and rigatoni al pesto with sun-dried tomatoes and pine nuts in pesto sauce. Exceptional food and a great wine list. Reservations recommended.

Country Fare - 2680 Middlefield Road, Palo Alto; (415) 326-3802. If you're planning a picnic along the trail, why not stop off here for sandwiches, salads, and drinks. Fresh organic ingredients are featured. Specialties include brie sandwiches, stuffed avocados, and other gourmet delights.

Maddalenas Cafe Bar- 544 Emerson Street, Palo Alto; (415) 326-6082. Fresh salmon, filet mignon, breast of chicken provençal, and veal piccata are among the specialties at this popular Silicon Valley restaurant. The impressive chandeliered main dining room is complimented by the art deco cafe featuring entertainment nightly. Reservations recommended.

Bella Mia - 14503 Big Basin Way, Saratoga: (408) 741-5115. Known for its pasta dishes, this romantic restaurant offers seating in the Victorian dining room or outdoors on the patio. Specialties include salmon ravioli in a tomato dill sauce, prawns, lobster and scallops with garlic butter sauce, and flatbread pizzas. Live jazz adds to the fun.

Bob's Oak Room - 945 The Alameda, San Jose; (408) 279-1585. As you probably guessed, the walls here are paneled in oak. The ribs are great and this is also a good stop for top sirloin or chicken brochettes. Place your order while having a drink in the bar and you'll be shown to your table when dinner is served. Ideal for the larger than average appetite.

Eulipia - 374 S. First Street, San Jose; (408) 280-1639. Brick walls, high ceilings, and "high concept" food make Eulipia a winner. Try the mesquite grilled salmon with caramelized shallots and basalmic vinaigrette, and black pepper fettucine with pesto, fresh tomatoes, and goat cheese. There's a great copper bar. Reservations recommended.

Hamburger Mary's - 170 W. St. John Street, San Jose; (408) 947-1667. Create your own omelet or order Hawaiian French toast at this popular brickwalled establishment. There's also a champagne brunch on Sunday.

La Foret - 21747 Bertram Road (Route G8), San Jose; (408) 997-3458. Located in a historic creekside hotel, this rustic French restaurant makes a great dinner choice. On the menu are ahi tuna grilled served in horseradish and thyme sauce and breast of duck roasted with madeira and morels. Reservations recommended.

Paradiso Delicatessen - 791 Auzeras Avenue, San Jose; (408) 295-6459. This Italian deli is perfect place to plan a picnic. A variety of lunch meats, including dry salamis, imported and domestic provolone, French bread, and chocolate chip cookies will keep your strength up on the trail.

The Bagelry - 320 Cedar Street, Santa Cruz; (408) 429-8049. Bagels here are served 20 different ways. Hummus, lox spread, cream cheese, olives, and green onions, vegetable cream cheese, and egg salad are just a few of your options. Fresh juices, gourmet coffee, and chai are also served in a relaxed setting.

India Joze - 1001 Center Street, Santa Cruz ; (408) 427-3554. In this multicultural age, India Joze is the place to find Near, Middle, and Far Eastern Cuisine. The Persian Wok offers chicken, lamb, or calamari in a mild pomegranate cream and fresh mint glaze. The same three choices are also available with Javan pesto in a fresh ginger basil, tamarind sauce. The Dragon is a tangy fresh mint and cilantro glaze on calamari or chicken.

Rosa's Rosticeria - 493B Lake Avenue, Santa Cruz; (408) 479-3536. Enjoy views of the harbor as you dine on excellent burritos, quesadillas, or spit-roasted chicken. The salsa bar is first rate and ribs are also served.

Zoccoli's Delicatessen - 1534 Pacific Avenue, Santa Cruz (408) 423-1711. The ultimate Italian deli offering a wide array of meat and meatless sandwiches served on sourdough rolls, with tortellini salad, pesto pasta salad, red potato salad, and homemade chocolate chip cookie bars. Add a Power Bar and a fruit drink and you're on your way.

The Veranda - 8041 Soquel Drive, Aptos; (408) 685-1881. American classics updated for the '90s make this restored Victorian restaurant south of Santa Cruz a good choice. Rack of lamb smoked, roasted, and marinated with buttermilk, mustard, garlic, and rosemary is popular as is the filet of salmon baked with a mustard herb crust and served with a three mustard vin blanc. Reservations recommended.

South Bay Walks

Walk #1: San Pedro Valley Park - Hazelnut Trail

Walking Easy Time
2½ hours

Nestled in the coastal foothills of Pacifica is 1,150-acre San Pedro Valley Park. Discovered by accident in 1769 by Spanish explorer Captain Gaspar de Portola, the Valley's fertile soil ultimately proved valuable in the Spanish mission system.

San Pedro Creek, flowing year round, was used as a trout farm in the 1950s and today harbors some of the country's last remaining steelhead. Located on the outskirts of this seaside community, the park offers the *Easy Walker* coastal views and chaparral-lined trails. Keep an eye out for red-tailed hawks and scrub jays.

There are no picnic or bathroom facilities on the hike, but they are available near the park's visitor center.

We recommend you reserve time to explore the visitor center located on the eastern end of the parking lot. It offers informative exhibits on the flora and fauna pertinent to this region and the greater Bay Area.

Directions: Drive southbound from San Francisco on Highway 101, and continue to head south on I-230 and State Highway 1. In the city of Pacifica, turn left off Highway 1 onto Linda Mar Blvd. After two miles this street dead ends into Oddstat Blvd. Turn right here, and signs for the park are straight ahead.

This easy walk explores foothills densely covered with thick coastal scrub intermixed with manzanita, chinquapin, and scatterings of California hazelnut trees. Come springtime, the four-and-a-half-mile loop is lined with pink hedge nettle and bursting with blue blossom, orange poppies, and wild mustard. The Hazelnut Trail is peaceful and particularly pleasing as a cool, misty, early morning walk.

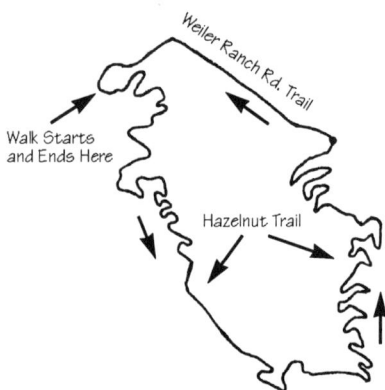

Walk Starts and Ends Here

Weiler Ranch Rd. Trail

Hazelnut Trail

Start: Just beyond and right of the visitor center is the trailhead for the Plaskon Nature Trail which is where you'll begin today's easy walk. The Hazelnut trailhead breaks right, fifteen yards after crossing San Pedro Creek, and marks your initial ascent through the foothills. The lush creekside and riparian environment dominated by dogwood and giant trillium, contrasts with the dryer chaparral community as you scale the trail's foothills.

Zigzagging up through dense foliage into an aromatic grove of towering eucalyptus trees, your trek along the Hazelnut Trail is lined with native shrubs, manzanita and low trees. Along the way enjoy panoramic views of the park, the community, and the Pacific. Several rest benches on the path are a welcome sight. They are perfect for a snack and views of the scenery below.

After leveling off near the eucalyptus grove, the Hazelnut Trail leads northeast through the chaparral wilderness and ends about a half mile east of your starting point.

Veer left on Weiler Road and complete your hike at the visitor center.

Walks #2 and #3: Memorial and Sam McDonald County Parks

The Santa Cruz mountain range's Memorial and Sam McDonald County parks are home to spectacular old-growth redwoods. There are no picnic facilities on either of these walks so plan on lunching in between exploring the two. Bathrooms and picnic tables are located near the ranger stations in each park.

Directions: South of San Francisco, the parks are accessed via State Highway 84 heading west off either Highway 101, Interstate 280, or State Highway 32 (Skyline Boulevard). If you're coming from the East Bay, take Interstate 880 south and cross the San Mateo Bridge (via State Highway 92) which intersects these highways.

Several miles west of La Honda, turn left onto Pescadero Road, and continue another mile to the Sam McDonald County Park entrance. Four miles further on is the entrance to Memorial County Park. There is a small parking fee in Memorial Park.

Walk #2: Memorial Park - Pomponio Trail

Walking Easy Time
2 hours

Established in 1924, commemorating the soldiers who died in World War I, Memorial Park is San Mateo's oldest county park. Many of the facilities within the park were erected in the 1930s by the WPA. While much of the surrounding wilderness was logged, this land was preserved for future campers, picnickers and, of course, *Easy Walkers*. Lofty coast redwoods provide a cool environment for hikers on warm summer days.

Enjoyable any time of day, Pomponio Trail is a pleasant, three-mile loop, ascending and descending adjoining ridges within the Santa Cruz mountain range. Although the elevation varies slightly, the contrast between the lush, moist flora of the redwoods and the dryer climate near the summit is striking. Vista-like views are few on this easy walk, but the immediate surroundings are intriguing.

Start: The Pomponio trailhead is located just across Pescadero Road from the Park's entrance. Lining your path are lush ferns and redwood sorrel or "wild shamrock" which help preserve the forest's moisture. The trail is conveniently marked with signs leading walkers through the lush hillside canyon. Winding up the hillside through the canyon, enjoy the consuming lushness. Baby blue eyes and redwood trillium brighten the moist earth while California hazelnut trees and their velvety soft leaves add to the forest's beauty. Don't be spooked by the bright yellow, slimy banana slugs populating this region.

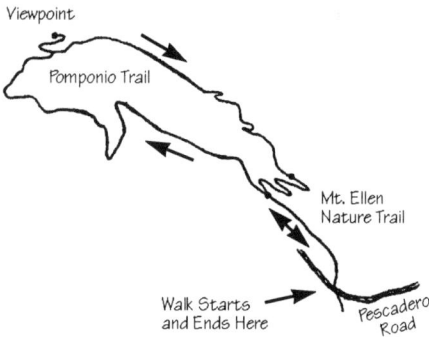

Viewpoint

Pomponio Trail

Mt. Ellen
Nature Trail

Walk Starts
and Ends Here

Pescadero
Road

Near the top, the park boundary directs the footpath over a wooden bridge toward the opposite ridge. Orange poppies and sticky monkey flower stand out vibrantly amid the chaparral and sandstone. Soon you'll approach a sign directing left towards a "scenic overlook." Only a five-minute detour, you may want to explore this spur path culminating in a tiny cul-de-sac surrounded by oaks. In the distance, smooth hills roll grandly towards the sea.

Backtrack to the beginning of the detour and continue left along the Pomponio Trail, heading toward the Ranger Station. On the way down take the lower path at the fork and switchback down, once more coursing through the redwoods to Pescadero Road.

Walk #3: Sam McDonald County Park - Big Tree Loop

Walking Easy Time
30 minutes

Adjacent Sam McDonald County Park, named after the Louisiana native and slave descendent who once owned this land, was recently opened to the public. An employee at Stanford University for over fifty years, McDonald gradually purchased land in this area. Upon his death, the land was left to the University. It was used only for recreational purposes, before ownership eventually passed to the county. This 850-acre refuge offers miles of pleasure-filled walks. We've chosen one of the best—short, yet unforgettable.

The Big Tree Loop is a brisk, one-mile jaunt through a hauntingly peaceful and verdant old-growth redwood preserve. Like the Pomponio Trail, this walk is well sign posted and easy to follow.

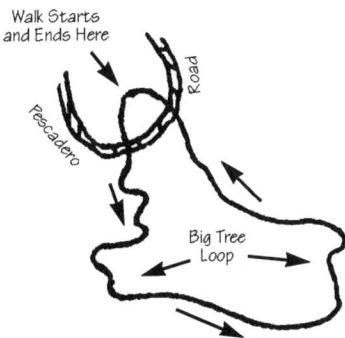

Start: Begin at the southern end of the parking lot, opposite the Ranger Station where you'll see a large, hollow redwood. The initial sign near this tree directs walkers across Pescadero Road where, on the other side, a narrow trail continues briefly before merging with the larger fire road. Fifty yards further on, the path breaks left onto the Big Tree Loop trail. This fern-lined pathway forges into a dense redwood region where thick trunks flank either side and ascend steeply to majestic heights. After mounting the wooden steps, keep a look out for a small fork branching left. This detour enters a little nook with a makeshift bench ideal for a quick snack or enjoying the cool calm of this serene area.

Return to the original path. Merge with the fire road and break left 50 yards further on, just beyond the dark green water tank. Marking your descent, this narrow path lures walkers into the thick enclosure of these massive trees. Walking through the virgin forest, you may have the tranquil enclave to yourself. Enjoy this fascinating territory where, depending on the time of year, pink sorrel blossoms or the bright burst of giant trillium add wondrous color to the dark green verdancy.

Stay left on the main trail and follow the signs towards Pescadero Road and the Ranger Station.

Walk #4: Huddart County Park - Crystal Springs Trail to Dean Trail

Walking Easy Time
3 hours

Public property since 1944 when James Huddart donated his land to the County of San Mateo, Huddart County Park shows how land abuse can be rectified. Originally these 973 acres were part of a larger 12,545-acre Spanish rancho. Between 1850 and 1860, however, the large coast redwoods met the growing demand for Gold Rush lumber. Logging virtually destroyed the redwoods on this site and what you see today is new growth taking place over the last century.

Directions: Huddart County Park lies alongside King's Mountain Road, nestled between State Highways 84 (Woodside Road) and 35 (Skyline Boulevard) in San Mateo County. After entering the park, turn left just beyond the ranger station, and follow signs (right) towards the Zwierlein Picnic Area.

Descending through canyons and skimming open ridges, today's refreshing walk leads through cool redwood groves and the mixed evergreen forests of the eastern Santa Cruz Mountains.

No bathrooms are located on the hike. Picnic facilities are available along the latter section of Dean Trail.

Start: To the right of the restroom is a smaller parking lot and the trailhead for today's walk. Veer left on this path, Crystal Springs Trail, toward Skyline Trail. Head along a series of switchbacks leading up the canyon. Here, colorful madrones, tanbark oak, and bay laurel trees gradually give way to stately coast redwoods as you head toward McGarvey Gulch Creek.

Cross two footbridges and at the junction with Richard's Road Trail begin ascending the opposite ridge. Thriving upon the moisture of McGarvey Gulch Creek, the redwoods provide a refreshingly cool environment for comfortable walking. Greenery abounds in a carpet of sorrel, ferns, and moss covered rocks and tree trunks.

Veer left at the sign reading: "Toyon Group .1". Shortly after this point you'll reach paved Toyon Road. Crystal Springs continues straight ahead, across the road.

Here, another switchback leads up the ridge. Find yourself gradually surrounded by coast live oak trees, tan bark oak, and red-hued madrones. You'll also see other varieties such as California black and blue oak trees.

Crystal

Springs

Trail

Walk Starts
and Ends Here

Dean Trail

At the first fork, proceed left. This is Dean Trail, a descending route leading walkers back towards park headquarters. On the way, you'll move once again from the dryer, mixed evergreen forest into lush redwood country.

Dean Trail crosses Archery Fire Road twice and rims Miwok, Madrone, and Werder picnic areas on its return. Turn right at the familiar Crystal Springs junction and follow it back to the lower parking lot.

Walk #5: Wunderlich County Park - Bear Gulch Trail to Madrone Trail to Redwood Trail to Meadow Trail and return on Alambique Trail

Walking Easy Time
1½ hours

The Costanoan Indians were the first to live here and utilize the eastern slopes now comprising Wunderlich County Park. White settlers arrived in the late 18th century and the region was turned to pastureland and denuded by loggers. This region's most notable 20th-century owner was San Francisco entrepreneur and coffee magnate, James A. Folger. He and his family kept the land in wilderness for more than five decades. They sold the property to Martin Wunderlich, the last private owner.

Because elevation varies slightly and there are many short, scenic loops to chose from, this area is perfect for walkers of all ages and abilities. Nine hundred and forty-two accessible acres of mixed woodlands and spacious grass clearings delight locals and visiting *Easy Walkers.*

Directions: From Highway 101 exit on State Highway 84 heading west toward Woodside. The park's entrance is located two miles west of Woodside on State Highway 84 in San Mateo County.

This hike is perfect for *Easy Walkers.* Grades are gradual, and the diverse terrain offers plenty of variety. The gardenlike setting is a big hit with parents. Bathrooms are situated at the western side of the parking lot, but nowhere along the route we've selected.

Start: The Bear Gulch trailhead is located at the western end of the parking lot. It begins with a short, half-mile switchback ascent through a mixed forested area including black oak, California hazelnut, and bay laurel trees. Fallen trees and branches, shrouded with dense cobwebs, give these woods an eerily unkempt feel. Loose dirt from the footpath dusts the lush green of sword and bracken fern.

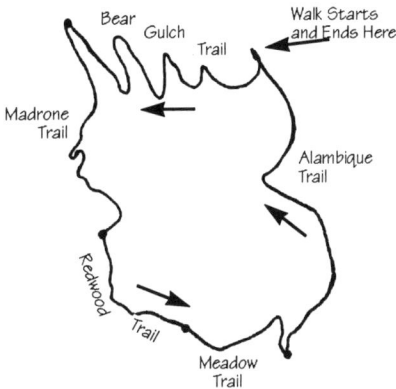

Coast redwoods add beauty to these woodlands, as you bear left onto Madrone Trail, the second leg of today's walk, towards Salamander Flat. For two-thirds of a mile you'll also see Douglas firs and tanbark oak on this trail before hitting upon Salamander Flat.

A level traverse, Madrone Trail continues across the ridge eventually merging left with Redwood Trail. This continues your leisurely stroll through a cool, dusky grove of these towering beauties before veering left on Meadow Trail.

Like the Madrone Trail, this one does not live up to its name; there is no meadow on Meadow trail. Instead, your path emerges from the redwood's cover onto an open path where colorful madrones and scented eucalyptus trees line the quarter of a mile to Alambique Trail.

Complete the loop after cutting left on Alambique Trail. This final leg journeys for three-quarters of a mile downward along the side of the ridge. On your final descent peninsula views filter through the valley and black oaks before returning to the parking lot.

Walk #6: Joseph D. Grant County Park - Hotel Trail to San Felipe Trail

Walking Easy Time
3½ hours

Forty miles of trails course through the 9,522 acres of grass and oak woodlands comprising Joseph D. Grant County Park. Situated in Halls Valley, a scenic stretch between two ridges in the Diablo Mountain Range east of Santa Clara Valley, this area was home to the Ohlone Indians before becoming part of a 15,000-acre Mexican land grant called *Rancho Canada de Pala* in 1839. A portion of the Rancho, sold off little by little to white settlers, was purchased by Adam Grant in 1880. Later, his son J.D. Grant purchased additional lands. A wealthy mercantile family, the Grants used the land for recreational purposes until 1972 when J.D.'s daughter passed away. Purchased by the county in 1975 and opened to the public in 1978, the area was deemed a wildlife sanctuary where biologists tried to reintegrate tule elk that once freely roamed here. Unfortunately most of the elk have migrated, but you are likely to see several wild European pigs in the area.

Directions: From Interstate 680 or U.S. Highway 101 take the Alum Rock Avenue exit east in San Jose and turn right on Mt. Hamilton Road. The park's entrance is another eight miles further on.

If you're already in San Jose, travel to Grant County Park via Capitol Expressway. Exit right, onto Quimby Road, and drive another five miles into the park.

Once in the park proceed to the furthest day use parking lot, near Stockman's picnic area, before reaching the campgrounds.

Today's trails form an oblong loop bordering an idyllic meadow laced by San Felipe Creek. The entire journey is approximately five miles, but there are several opportunities to shorten today's walk via Barn and Corral trails which cut through the meadow. You can also lengthen it by venturing on to Eagle Lake. Picnic facilities and bathrooms are found only in Stockman's picnic area. There is little shade through much of the walk so consider wearing a hat in summer. You will also be entering livestock territory; watch for cattle, and remember to close gates behind you.

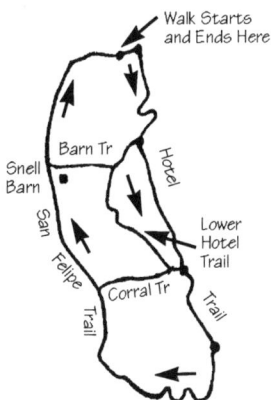

Walk Starts and Ends Here
Snell Barn
Barn Tr
Hotel
San Felipe Trail
Corral Tr
Trail
Lower Hotel Trail

Start: Find the Hotel trailhead at the far eastern end of Stockman's Picnic Area. Veer right onto the wide multipurpose trail, pass through the cattle guard, and begin your journey along San Felipe Creek's eastern shore. Relatively straightforward, Hotel Trail makes for a leisurely stroll through soft and golden grassy pastures which turn a rich green come springtime. Oak clusters spot the foothills to your left while spring and summer wildflowers color the meadow on your right.

Upon reaching the first fork, you can go either way: Hotel Trail is graded and therefore a tad more challenging, while Lower Hotel trail, veering right, bypasses the hill and skims the meadow. Along Lower Hotel Trail you can see, isolated far across the meadow, the picturesque Snell Barn. Walkers on the lower trail, lined with yellow star thistle, can shorten today's walk by taking the Barn Trail detour through the meadow to San Felipe Trail.

A similar option is available another half mile further on, at the junction with Corral Trail. Here the two Hotel trails merge again. Corral Trail cuts through the meadow and returns to Stockman's Picnic Area via San Felipe Trail.

Continuing along Hotel Trail the path crosses a small tributary, where sycamore and bay laurel trees blend with valley and coast live oak, and begins a winding ascent.

A half mile later turn right at the junction with Canada de

Pala Trail. (If you are feeling good and have additional time, you may want to venture straight ahead on Hotel Trail. Scenic Eagle Lake is another mile further on and is great for picnicking.) Veering right at the junction, walkers will continue an eighth of a mile towards refreshing San Felipe Creek where verdant foliage offers a welcome contrast to the surrounding foothills.

As the trail ascends the foothills opposite the creek towards San Felipe Trail, lush shrubbery gives way to a dryer woodland dominated by blue oak and Oregon white oak trees. San Felipe Trail ventures north another mile and a half along the meadow's western edge. From this side, hikers can see Snell Barn up close before reaching the paved road approaching the park's campground area. The trail continues along the left hand side of the road, but it's easier to stay on the paved section leading walkers straight to Stockman's Picnic Area.

Walk #7: Almaden Quicksilver County Park - New Almaden Trail to Hacienda Trail along Capehorn Pass to Mine Hill Trail to Hacienda Trail to No Name Trail

Walking Easy Time
4 hours

All shafts and tunnels have been closed in this 3,600-acre park, originally the site of the first quicksilver mine in North America. Indians, aware of the cinnabar located in these hills, used the mineral for face painting long before the Spanish arrived. The Spanish "discovered" cinnabar, the most important ore in mercury or quicksilver, at Sutters fort in 1845. They named the mine Nuevo Almaden after the Almaden mines in Spain. After it had been mined for over a century, the property was acquired by the Santa Clara Department of Parks and Recreation in 1970 and opened to the public in 1975 as the county's second largest park. Thirty miles of hiking and equestrian trails run throughout the park, best avoided in the summer months when extreme heat might make for uncomfortable hiking. Come springtime, however, views of the valley extend for miles and are framed by native and exotic wildflowers brought from Europe by the Spanish and Cornish miners who worked these hills.

Directions: Interstate 280 and Highway 101 from San Francisco both lead south towards San Jose. If on Highway 101, take I-280 west when you get to San Jose. From I-280 take State Highway 87 and exit on the Almaden Expressway turning right. Follow Almaden all the way until it dead ends and turn right. At the second stop sign turn left and then make a quick right on Mockingbird Hill Lane entering the park.

While you are exploring the eastern section of this park, various peaks along these trails offer unique Santa Clara Valley vantage points. Walkers be warned, this one is *not* easy. Hills are quite steep in parts. Only attempt this walk if you feel you're in excellent shape. Bathrooms and picnic areas are located near the parking lot, and remember to bring plenty of water.

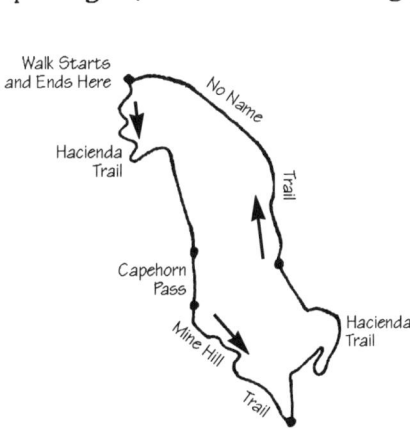

Walk Starts and Ends Here

No Name

Hacienda Trail

Trail

Capehorn Pass

Mine Hill

Trail

Hacienda Trail

Start: Your walk through Almaden Quicksilver begins along a brief section of New Almaden Trail. Located at the southern end of the lot is the trailhead and a small post providing a brief history of the park. The path heads into a mixed grove veering southwest before it merges with Hacienda Trail. On this path, additional posts elaborate upon the park's past. Along the way you'll learn how Native Americans put local flora to use.

Exit the grove and turn left on Hacienda Trail. Here is an extended open ascent through dry brush colored with orange sticky monkey flower. Look back to see an impressive vista of the Santa Clara Valley. Ascending further, past valley and black oak trees, walkers can see downtown San Jose and the Diablo Range opposite the valley.

After reaching an initial summit the trail dips and rises on its way to Capehorn Pass. Turn right at the Pass and descend towards Mine Hill Trail; this route offers a brief northwesterly glimpse of lofty peaks, deep crevices, and windy routes leading into the heart of this mining region.

Make a soft left at the end of the Pass where Mine Hill Trail leads you down a dusty, loose dirt path, through coyote brush and blue oak trees. Not too steep, the descent is long and gradual.

Just beyond the signposted restricted area, make a hard left onto Hacienda Trail. The first half of this ascending slope is gradual, like Mine Trail, and not too tiring. Yellow star thistle lines the path and sycamore trees make an appearance among the oaks. Almaden Reservoir shimmers behind you in the distance.

The last portion (200 yards) of Hacienda Trail, before striking right onto No Name Trail, is difficult. Steep ascending and descending grades with loose dirt make for lots of pauses and slippery footing. Be careful along this section.

The initial stretch on No Name Trail offers a welcome sight after the last bit on Hacienda Trail. Turning into a slight descent, this grassy, less densely foliated eastern slope provides clear valley views before reaching the base of the hill. The pathway then swerves left, traversing the rolling, lower portion of these foothills which border the residential neighborhoods of Almaden, and eventually exits, after a mile and a half, onto the eastern end of the parking lot.

Walk #8: Henry Coe State Park - Monument Trail to Northern Heights Route to Frog Lake to Middle Ridge Trail to Fish Trail and back on Corral Trail

Walking Easy Time
5 hours

Off the beaten path in southeast Santa Clara Valley, not many visitors make it to Henry Coe State Park. An oak woodland wilderness with grassy ridges and rugged canyons, this hidden gem was purchased in 1883 by pioneer rancher Henry Coe. He was preceded by Spanish explorers who introduced cattle grazing to the property initially inhabited by the Ohlone and Yokut Indians.

Today, with over 68,000 acres and 200 miles of trails, Henry Coe is the largest State Park in northern California. Plan your visit in the springtime when the hillsides are vibrantly colored with buttercups, fiddlenecks, and redmaids. In the summer months this area is extremely hot, a high fire risk, and best to be avoided.

Spur Trail
Middle Ridge Trail
Frog Lake
Northern Heights Route
Monument Trail
Trail
Fish
Corral Trail
Walk Starts and End Here

Directions: Heading south on Highway 101 from San Jose, take the East Dunne exit in Morgan Hill and continue east. Drive an additional three miles uphill and, from there, follow the narrow and windy, ten-mile course into the park.

From the grassy hillsides on your way to Frog Lake, the panoramic views atop Middle Ridge, and the deep riparian canyons on Fish Trail, walkers experience six and a half miles (just a fraction of this park's great expanse) of pure wilderness. Restrooms and picnic facilities are located near the visitor center. Be sure to bring plenty of water.

Start: A short jaunt on Corral Trail, just across the road from the visitor center, leads walkers to the Monument trailhead which bears left and ascends open grasslands shaded by oak and buckeye trees.

After crossing wide Northern Heights Route, remain on Monument Trail. Carrying hikers up through stands of valley oak, knobcone pine, bay laurel, and scatterings of manzanita, this smaller trail parallels and eventually merges with Northern Heights Route. You'll head left and begin the long descent toward Frog Lake. Although the path is wide, proceed cautiously on the steeper stretches.

Frog Lake is more like a large pond resting at the base of Middle Ridge's western slope. You're likely to find reflected in its still waters, images of black birds perched on full bald trunks jutting from its depths. Traverse the lake's eastern shore and a small spur trail leads walkers upwards, alongside a tributary, through grasslands, and out onto Northern Heights Route.

Turn right on the wide, level walkway, and proceed another quarter to half a mile before bearing right on Middle Ridge Trail.

This much narrower path begins with a gradual grade as it heads south atop Middle Ridge. Pine, valley, and California black oak trees stud grassy clearings. From here you can see the park's unyielding expanse in all directions.

Within a short time, ascents and descents progressively become more frequent and challenging as dense manzanita bushes begin crowding out the grasslands.

Begin your descent and move out of the scrub into wooded areas. Fish Trail ultimately veers right for the final two miles of today's trek.

Your route switches back through two canyons. The moisture from Little Fork Coyote Creek and a smaller tributary creates a riparian environment of willows, alders, and oaks.

Upon ascending the second canyon, your course across the bald ridge is intersected by Pacheco Route. Proceed on the other side (Springs Trail) for a short way and bear right on Corral Trail for the remaining half-mile trek to the visitor center.

Walk #9: Mount Madonna County Park - Bayview Trail

Walking Easy Time
1 hour

Sequoia Sempervirens, or more commonly, coast redwoods reach soaring heights on Mount Madonna while blending with a thriving evergreen forest along its western slope. On the mountain's eastern face, a varied terrain of oak trees and grass lands descend into Santa Clara County. Named after the Blessed Virgin by poet, Hiram Wentworth, the land was originally a popular Ohlone hunting and gathering site. When the Spanish assumed ownership the mountain became part of the much larger *Rancho Las Animas*. Cattle baron Henry Miller purchased this verdant area for commercial grazing, but reserved Mount Madonna for his family's summer retreats.

While today's walk explores Mount Madonna's western slopes, we recommend driving to the summit where you can see the foundations of Miller's four summer homes and an anomalous yet intriguing family of white fallow deer—a gift from William Randolph Hearst.

Directions: Located ten miles west of Gilroy, follow State Highway 152 west off Highway 101. Wind along 152 towards the summit and when you near Mount Madonna Inn, bear northeast on Pole Line Road leading into the park.

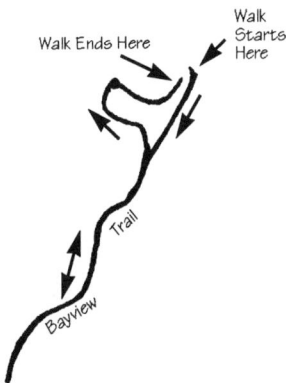

This is a short, pleasant stroll, allowing plenty of time to explore other interesting sights within the park. The trail name is slightly deceiving as the dense forest obstructs views of Monterey Bay, but the flora is richly varied and equally interesting. There are no bathroom or picnic facilities along this trail, but they are found at numerous other spots around the park. You can find them by consulting the free map available at the information kiosk.

Start: From the Horse Trailer Parking Area, proceed across the main road, backtracking about ten yards toward the park entrance. A post on the west side of the road with a yellow horseshoe marks the beginning of Bayview Trail. Tan bark oak trees prominently flank the walkway at the beginning of the path, and stunning pink foxgloves add a delicate presence during the summer months.

Near the park entrance, the sloping trail enters a brief clearing with colorful manzanita, coyote brush, and orange sticky monkey flower. This elfin forest soon gives way to tall, red-hued madrones and cool, thick redwoods. California hazelnut trees with smooth velvety leaves sprout atop a varied forest floor of sorrel, sword and bracken fern, snowberry, two-eyed violets, and wild roses.

Three quarters of a mile into the hike, when the trail narrows and the adjacent canyon recedes steeply below, you'll approach Highway 152. If you don't feel like returning just yet, exit the trail at Highway 152 and head west several yards where you'll see the monument commemorating Henry Heckler. Heckler Pass is named for the county supervisor who guided Mount Madonna's transition from private estate to county park.

The second half of the walk returns along the same path, but veers left at the wooden post. This detour, traversing the opposite ridge, creates a slightly longer return, offering open views of Watsonville and, in the distance, Monterey Bay.

Turn right at the next fork and finish up the hike with a quiet stroll shaded by redwoods and scented eucalyptus.

Walk #10: Castle Rock State Park - Saratoga Gap Trail to Ridge Trail

Walking Easy Time
4 hours

Located atop a western ridge of the 25-million year-old Santa Cruz Mountain Range, Castle Rock State Park is known for its unusual rock formations, craggy rock outcroppings, and sheer sandstone cliffs offering spectacular vistas.

No one knows if Indians inhabited this specific region, but mortars and spearheads found here suggest this area was part of their nomadic life. From the Civil War era through the turn of the century, the ridge was settled by farming and logging families. By the early 20th century this spot had become a popular tourist site. Among the region's enthusiasts was Russell Varlay, who sought to preserve this scenic enclave. After he died in 1959, 27 acres were purchased with the help of donations made in his behalf. More land was acquired and Castle Rock ultimately opened to the public in 1968 with 513 acres. It has progressively grown to 3,600 spectacular acres with 32 miles of hiking trails leading through bowled meadows, across evergreen forests, and up along open sandstone ridges.

Directions: North of Los Gatos and east of Saratoga, Castle Rock State Park is found off State Highway 35, just two and a half miles south of the junction with State Highway 9 in eastern Santa Cruz County. Parking is plentiful on the road outside of the park.

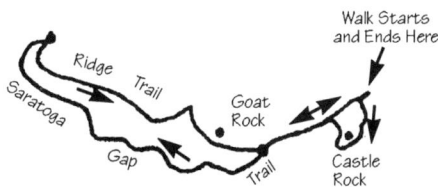

Today *Easy Walkers* tour two popular rock formations, a scenic waterfall, and hike along open ridges with awesome views and beautiful forests. The climate here is generally cool, as the forest provides plenty of shade and clearings are ventilated by a refreshing Pacific breeze. If you wish to shorten today's walk, plan on skipping the initial detour to Castle Rock. Later, take the small spur trail providing a shortcut midway through the walk.

Bathrooms are located near the parking lot at the entrance and in the campground area. Picnic facilities are also located near the campground. You can also improvise a romantic feast overlooking the Santa Cruz Mountains at Goat Rock, near your journey's end.

Start: Several trails begin at the west end of the parking lot. We strongly recommend taking the brief, half-mile detour towards Castle Rock, one of several sandstone formations found in this unique park. Enter the lush evergreen forest via the left hand trail. Here, stately coast redwoods and Douglas firs share the landscape with tanbark oak trees. Red-hued madrones also brighten the landscape. A cluster of stone formations lead the way to Castle Rock. Once you arrive, spend time in this shady area exploring the nooks and crannies of this popular site.

Return trails lead to the parking lot or Saratoga Gap Trail, where you'll begin the better part of today's hike. Heading west on Saratoga Gap Trail, continue alongside the petite creek flanked by towering redwood, willow, and big leaf maple trees. Boulders dot the area and occasionally obstruct the path. Be prepared to maneuver along the descent.

A three-quarters-of-a-mile journey leads to Castle Rock Falls Overlook. Skillful mountain climbers are often seen scaling the cliffs adjacent to the falls. On clear days, the falls panorama also includes glimpses of the Pacific.

Continuing along Saratoga Gap Trail, you'll soon emerge from the cool cover of the shady forest onto a chaparral clearing, colorfully lined with manzanita and bright orange sticky monkey flower. The footpath, carved along the side of the ridge, traverses a mile-long stretch offering canyon, mountain, and Pacific views.

For *Easy Walkers* wishing to head back early, a short-cut, via a small spur trail, runs from the Saratoga Gap across to Ridge Trail. Diehard walkers forge ahead along the Saratoga Gap Trail which eventually veers inland. Soon, you'll reach the campground and nearby picnic area. You may wish to stop here for lunch.

Before entering the campground area, the well-signposted Ridge Trail veers right (sharply) in the opposite direction. This return jaunt forges though dense clusters of colorful madrones, fragile hazelnut, California black, and prickly coast live oak trees. Unfortunately, echoes from the nearby shooting range disturb the serenity of this leg of the trail.

After a mile, turn right on the footpath (still Ridge Trail) leading toward Goat Rock. A popular climbing spot, Goat Rock is also a warm and pleasant place to rest or lunch while watching daring individuals work the granite slabs.

From Goat Rock, continue a short distance on Ridge Trail before merging with the familiar Saratoga Gap Trail. Exercise caution, as jutting stones make the brief descent slightly difficult. Take it slow!

Ridge Trail eventually empties onto Saratoga Gap Trail where you'll turn left, heading east up the lushly shaded canyon towards civilization.

Walk #11: Big Basin Redwoods State Park - Skyline to the Sea Trail to Sequoia Trail

Walking Easy Time
3 hours

Fifteen-hundred-year-old coast redwoods, the prominent feature of Big Basin State Park, soar to majestic heights in this magnificent enclave of the Santa Cruz Mountain Range. Prior to 1769, when Spanish explorers first sighted the land, Native Americans hunted here for acorns and small game but declined to settle the region for religious reasons: they maintained a kind of supernatural regard for the massive redwoods. They also showed common sense: Big Basin was once largely populated with grizzly bears which they thought best to avoid.

At the height of the Gold Rush, Big Basin became an immensely popular logging region. Contentious citizens, horrified by the potential devastation, banded together in 1900 to form the Sempervirens Club (which later became the still active Sempervirens Fund) fighting for the land's restoration and preservation. Their success has been a gift to all of us. In 1902, the State of California acquired 2,500 acres of land. These numbers have grown over the century to cover an expanse of more than 19,000 acres.

Meanwhile, there is no lack of space available to visitors of

Big Basin. Eighty miles of hiking trails grace this spectacular park's mountains and valleys.

Directions: To reach Big Basin Redwoods State Park, take State Highway 236 (Big Basin Highway) west off State Highway 9 in Santa Cruz County. There's no missing the park entrance.

Today's hike, beginning just west of park headquarters, forms a wide loop extending north, along Skyline to the Sea Trail, and returns southeast to park headquarters via Sequoia Trail. A nice late afternoon hike, the park is cool and less crowded at this time of day. You also pass through several campground areas at dusk when campfires are freshly lit.

Start: Find the trailhead for the Sea to Skyline Trail by taking any of the spur paths leading west from park headquarters. Bear right when you hit the trail. Running, as the name suggests, from the Skyline to the Sea, the official skyline trailhead begins in Castle Rock State Park (see p. 168) and ends at Waddell Beach. Your course proceeds through the redwood section of this 37-mile trail. Paralleling Opal Creek, the trail courses through a forest of towering redwoods, huckleberry, and tanbark oak trees. Nearly as popular as the redwoods, tan bark oaks also faced widespread destruction. Their tannin was coveted by tanneries located in the county earlier in this century.

The pathway along the creek is worn and often vague, with spur trails leading in various directions. Most return to the main trail. Simply proceed ahead in a northerly direction keeping an eye out for reassuring signposts.

When the trail meets the paved North Escape Road, backtrack slightly, crossing the road, and connect onto Sequoia Trail.

Traveling north for a quarter of a mile, the trail then swerves southeast, traversing the side of the ridge. The canyon slopes steeply on your right as you climb to a higher elevation.

When you reach Big Basin Highway cross this well-traveled thoroughfare with care. Sequoia Trail continues on the other side. Switchback down a bit and arrive at Slippery Rock. As the name suggests, the trail proceeds along a relatively flat, slick, rock surface. Use caution, especially when wet. Near the bottom, turn right before reaching the paved road.

Your route parallels this road which connects with several campgrounds. A level, mile-and-a-half traverse remains as you weave through redwood stands and campgrounds on your way back to park headquarters.

Walk #12: Loch Lomond Recreation Area - Big Trees Nature Trail to Highlands Trail to Loch View Trail to Maclaren Trail

Walking Easy Time
3 hours

Off the beaten path, Loch Lomond Recreation Area is hidden snugly in the Santa Cruz Mountains, awaiting those desiring a spectacular wilderness and minimal crowds. Boaters and fishermen enjoy viewing this beautiful watershed from the reservoir's center while *Easy Walkers* traverse an open ridge and explore the second-growth (this area was logged in the late 1800 and early 1900s), mixed-evergreen hillsides sloping towards the private coves of Loch Lomond Reservoir.

Today the watershed is owned by the City of Santa Cruz Water Department. In addition to building the earth filled dam containing the reservoir, they are also responsible for preservation of the region after many years of abuse under private ownership. Walking through the area, you'll encounter a wilderness similar to the one known by the Zayante Indians, a subtribe of the Ohlones, who originally inhabited this area. The Loch Lomond Recreation Area is only open March 1st through September 15th.

Directions: Take State Highway 9 northeast from Santa Cruz. Several miles north of Felton, head east off Highway 9 onto Glen Arbor. (Be patient finding your way to Loch Lomond; just when you begin to think you're lost, another sign for the recreation area will appear.) At the first large junction continue driving east on Quail Hollow. Quail Hollow dead ends at a T-intersection where you'll turn left onto Zayante Road. Soon another sign for Loch Lomond directs you left onto Lompico Road. The road narrows as it winds through residential neighborhoods. Soon you're on West Drive, which leads straight into the park. There is a small parking fee. Ask at the kiosk for a general area map and for the booklet detailing the Big Trees Nature Trail (there may be an additional charge). After driving past the kiosk make the first right turn and park in the upper lot.

The base for today's walk, Glen Corrie Picnic Area has tables pleasantly scattered within the forest and bathrooms nearby. Today's route takes you through the forest towards an open ridge where you'll see panoramic views of the entire watershed wilderness. Completing the loop, *Easy Walkers* descend towards the Reservoir and traverse its shores back to Glen Corrie. Consider making this a morning trek as the afternoon heat on exposed Highlands Trail can be intense.

Start: The initial leg of today's walk leads you along a portion of the Big Trees Nature Trail, a self guiding loop. This short detour, before venturing on Highlands Trail, sets the tone of the hike. It points out some of the trees you'll witness in this semi evergreen forest, as well as smaller plants, wildflowers, fauna, and sounds to listen for.

Bear right when crossing the fire road (Highlands Trail) for the second time. (There is no sign.) This ascending trail leads past Douglas firs and tanbark oak, towards the mountain crest overlooking Loch Lomond Reservoir. Steep in parts, this initial section of the Highlands Trail can be hot in the summer due to the lack of shade. Banked on both sides with masses of yellow

Scotch broom, the trek to the top rewards hikers with grand views of the shimmering blue Reservoir below.

From this vantage point, Highlands Trail begins its gradual, winding descent through now shaded wilderness. Firs, madrones, and coast live oak initially filter the sunlight and share the territory with coast redwoods, hazelnut, and huckleberry trees, as you journey towards the Loch's shore. In the cove, picnic tables overlook the reservoir and there's a restroom if needed.

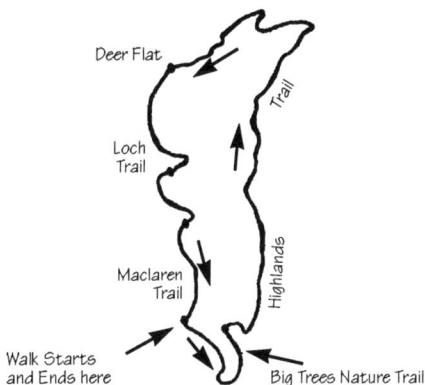

Swerving left along Highlands Trail, proceed straight ahead for your return trek on Loch View Trail, paralleling the reservoir's eastern shoreline. While walking, watch boaters paddling or fishing for rainbow trout, largemouth bass, and green sunfish. You may also catch sight of caspian terns swooping down to catch their prey. Grey tree stumps, once submerged, dot the shore.

Near Huckleberry Cove, the trail becomes trickier. After reaching the fork, take the left-hand path uphill. This trail thins out as you head into the forest. Follow it until you reach the point where the trail appears to dead end. From here improvise a 10 to 20 yard path (right) through the trees toward the reservoir. Look for the narrow, worn, footpath and you're back on track.

Head left, and follow the trail inland as it undulates through woodland brush. Listen closely and you may hear an acorn woodpecker or red shafted flicker working diligently away. Here you'll enter a grove of lofty redwoods and fragrant bay laurels.

At the next junction veer left and complete today's hike on Maclaren Trail. Pass through a mix of tanbark and coast live oak trees, laurels, and madrones before leaving via the lower portion of the Glen Corrie picnic area. Follow the paved road to the upper parking lot.

Walk #13: Henry Cowell State Park - Redwood Loop to Pipeline Road to Eagle Creek Trail to Pine Trail to the Observation Deck to Ridge Fire Road to Rincon Fire Road to River Trail and back along the Redwood Loop

Walking Easy Time
3½ hours

Henry Cowell came to the Bay Area from Massachusetts in 1849 with dreams of gold. Instead he made his fortune in limestone, ultimately gaining ownership of a big chunk of Santa Cruz County. The Santa Cruz campus of the University of California now lives on his former ranch, and Cowell's son donated this section of land to the state of California in his father's name. Today Henry Cowell State Park offers an 1800-acre recreational wilderness to horseback riders, bicyclists, and of course *Easy Walkers.*

Directions: From the city of Santa Cruz, drive north on State Highway 9. The park's entrance is located on the right just before the town of Felton.

Highway 9 can also be reached via State Highway 35 in San Mateo County. From State Highway 17, take the Scotts Valley exit and follow the signs toward Felton. From here the park is only a short drive south on Highway 9.

Once inside, park in the Redwood Grove Parking Area.

Today's walk is a five mile loop beginning and ending in a magnificent old growth redwood preserve. From the banks of San Lorenzo Creek ascend toward the summit and observation deck where you'll enjoy a very different landscape. Restrooms are located in the Redwood Grove parking lot and at the observation deck. Picnic facilities are found near the parking lot.

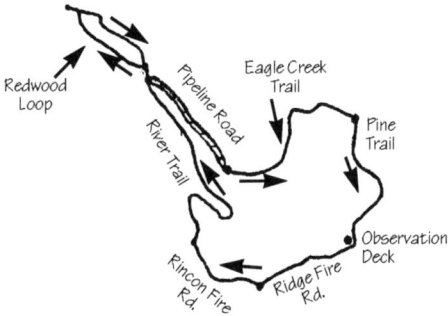

Walk Starts
and Ends Here

Redwood
Loop

Pipeline Road

River Trail

Eagle Creek
Trail

Pine
Trail

Observation
Deck

Rincon Fire
Rd.

Ridge Fire
Rd.

Start: Your course through Henry Cowell Redwoods begins along the southwestern (right) strand of the Redwood Loop. This area, once part of (county owned) Welch's Big Trees Resort, has long been a hit with visitors. (You can purchase a small leaflet at the nature center explaining the various trees and natural features of this area.) In addition to the redwoods, discover aromatic California bay laurels, and stately Douglas firs. The forest floor is carpeted with ferns, redwood sorrel, and occasionally Western azalea, wild ginger, or blooming thimble berry.

Exit the Redwood Loop at marker thirteen and follow the wide trail to paved Pipeline Road. Turn left here, dipping beneath the railroad underpass. Follow San Lorenzo Creek for a short distance before intersecting left on Eagle Creek Trail.

This trail marks the only ascent on today's walk. Paralleling Eagle Creek, the path forges through a mixed evergreen forest of coast live oaks, Douglas firs, and madrones. Keep an eye out for ponderosa pines which don't usually grow at this low elevation. Wooden steps are found near the summit of this trail which has several steep sections.

Shortly after crossing the creek via a wooden bridge, the pathway turns from loose dirt to thick sand, and Eagle Creek intersects with Pine Trail. Turn right (no sign) and traverse the nearly exposed ridge.

At this elevation (800 feet), chaparral has, for the most part, replaced the mixed evergreen forest. Instead of firs you'll find an elfin forest of yerba santa, manzanita, chamise, and knobcone pine. Heavy sand can make this section a slow and awkward traverse.

Signs direct you to the observation deck, an elevated, cement block providing panoramic views of surrounding peaks.

Your return hike begins on Ridge Fire Road. After a half mile of sand and thicket, cross Pipeline Road, and turn right, through stately redwoods, onto Rincon Fire Road.

This road descends through much of the same foliage. At the next junction, veer left on the smaller River Trail, rather than heading back to Pipeline Road.

Following signs for the picnic area, River Trail switchbacks down towards the San Lorenzo River. Crossing several wooden bridges, the trail, after a few steep descents, parallels the river where lush willow, cottonwood, and sycamores line the bank. California hazelnuts also are found along this path which meets Pipeline Road at the railroad underpass.

At the first signpost, turn right off Pipeline and head back into the redwood grove. Make your way to marker thirteen and then follow the right hand path, passing some of the grove's tallest redwoods, before returning to the park's nature center.

INDEX TO WALKS

South Bay

Index

For Credit Card ORDERS ONLY - call toll-free
1-800-669-0773
For Information - call 510-530-0299

Our books are available in many bookstores. If you have difficulty finding them, you can order directly from Gateway Books by sending check or money order to:

Gateway Books, 2023 Clemens Road, Oakland CA 94602

Walking Easy in the Austrian Alps $10.95.......................... _____

Walking Easy in the French Alps $11.95............................._____

Walking Easy in the Italian Alps $11.95.............................._____

Walking Easy in the San Francisco Bay Area $11.95....... _____

Walking Easy in the Swiss Alps $10.95............................._____

Postage & Handling

First book.............................$1.90   _____

Each additional book..........1.00   _____

California residents add 8% sales tax   _____

Total $ _____

( ) I enclose my check or money order
( ) Please charge my credit card

Visa   Master Card   American Express

#_____Exp. Date _____

Name on Card _____

Telephone (   )_____

Please ship to:

Name_____

Address_____

City/State/Zip_____

Our books are shipped bookrate. Please allow 2 - 3 weeks for delivery. If you are not satisfied, the price of the book(s) will be refunded in full. (U. S. funds for all orders, please.)

We want your comments, your criticisms and your suggestions of additional walks, excursions and accommodations to include in future editions. Please mail them to us at the above address, fax them to (510) 530-0497 or e-mail them to donmerwin@aol.com